**AFRICAN HISTORICAL DICTIONARIES**
**Edited by Jon Woronoff**

# Historical Dictionary

## of

# THE GAMBIA

by

## HARRY A. GAILEY

African Historical Dictionaries, No. 4

## The Scarecrow Press, Inc.

## Metuchen, N. J.      1975

Ref
DT
509.5
G13

Library of Congress Cataloging in Publication Data

Gailey, Harry A
    Historical dictionary of the Gambia.

    (African historical dictionaries ; no. 4)
    Bibliography:  p.
    1.  Gambia--History--Dictionaries.  I.  Title.
II.  Series.
DT509.5.G34        966'.51'003        75-5882
ISBN 0-8108-0810-2

Manufactured in the United States of America
Copyright 1975 by Harry A. Gailey

For

L. A. B. and L. E. B.

with gratitude for R. J. B.

## CONTENTS

## EDITOR'S FOREWORD

Although the Gambia is one of Africa's most artificial states geographically, it has nevertheless become very much of a political reality and would doubtlessly be listed among the more successful experiences in nation-building. A narrow sliver of land along the river that gives it sustenance, the Gambia resulted from a long history of conflict among the European colonial powers that almost ended with its disappearance. This history is particularly well traced by Professor Gailey, who also gives considerable insight as to why this "improbable" nation is now doing so well and has shown less eagerness than ever at forming part of a Senegambian entity.

From the outset, the African Historical Dictionaries have done more than just compile facts and information more or less readily available elsewhere. They have always gone a step further than the general literature in time, and often also in depth. The Gambian dictionary has been particularly successful in this by adding a broad analysis of post-independence history to the better known colonial past. And this has been done in a fascinating and absorbing fashion.

The task of the student, researcher and librarian has been facilitated by the comprehensive introductory essay that clearly places the Gambia in its historical, political and geographical context. The extensive chronology simplifies understanding of the whole historical period. The very complete annotated and classified bibliography makes it particularly easy to find additional material on specific subjects.

The Scarecrow Press was most fortunate in having as the author of this volume the same scholar who produced the only major study of the modern Gambia, Harry A. Gailey. After a lengthy stay in the country and considerable research, in 1964 he published <u>A History of the Gambia</u>, a book widely used in the school system there. Presently professor of history at San Jose State University, he has continued his research and writing in the young state, including numerous articles and essays. Now, a decade after his authoritative work appeared, Professor Gailey has summed up the body of historical knowledge and brought the story up to date in this dictionary.

Jon Woronoff
Series Editor

# INTRODUCTION

The tiny Republic of the Gambia is situated in the extreme western portion of the African continent surrounded on three sides by Senegal. The boundaries of the Gambia are completely artificial, having nothing to do with natural ethnic or geographic lines of demarcation. They were first drawn in 1889 during a meeting of French and British delegates in Paris, and were only slightly modified by later survey parties. The boundaries thus agreed upon satisfied both European governments and were meant to be only temporary since both parties were convinced that eventually there would be an exchange of the Gambia. For a variety of reasons, no transfer ever took place, and thus the third of a million Gambians are constrained to live today in a country whose limits are roughly ten kilometers distant from either side of the Gambia River. These lines exclude the Gambia from free access to its natural hinterland and divide the Gambian Wolof, Jola, Mandingo, and Fulbe people from their kinsmen in Senegal.

The present day boundaries of the Gambia present specific problems for the historian. Much of the history of the Gambia was not confined to the narrow serpentine state, but extended over the broad savannah and sahel areas that today comprise Senegal. This is particularly true of the period extending from the 13th through 16th centuries when the Gambia Valley was being populated by a series of complex migrations. Although little is known of the specifics, the Wolof, Mandingo, and Fulbe people established themselves in different sections of the Senegambia and there created first village- or clan-based polities and finally large kingdoms. These state building processes were still going on when the first European traders came to the Senegambian coast. By the opening of the 17th century, however, large complex states had been created throughout the region with kings, advisors, bureaucracies, and armed forces. The economic basis of each of these states was village oriented agriculture, although trade was important, particularly for those persons who lived near the rivers or close by a hinterland trade route.

1

European contact with the Gambia region dates to 1455 when the Portuguese first entered the estuary of the river. For over a century they maintained intermittent contacts with the area, unchallenged by any European rival. During this period a number of Portuguese chose to settle in the Gambia and the government and the church sponsored missionary activities among the Mandingo. However, the Gambia was never an important trading entrepôt and the Portuguese had decided to concentrate their efforts elsewhere along the west coast even before their trading monopoly was brought under attack by other European states. During the early 17th century, few Portuguese traders came to the Gambia on a regular basis. By the 18th century, the Portuguese interlude was only dimly remembered by the people of the Gambia, and the Portuguese left behind nothing of permanence.

The latter 16th century witnessed the continental rivalries of European states which were invariably transformed into worldwide conflicts. During the next two centuries, England, France, and Holland vied with one another for dominance in the world's mercantile trade. Transferred to the Senegambia region, these European quarrels disturbed the general peace, lowered profits, and ultimately prevented any one state from gaining a monopoly of the area's trade. At this juncture it is important to note that the Senegambia was not an area possessing great amounts of ivory, timber, pepper, or gold, and thus was by-passed by the major thrust of European trade in favor of more lucrative areas such as the Gold Coast. Nevertheless, there were trading companies active in the Gambia from 1598 onward. As the slave trade became more important, European investment in ships, fixed goods, and trading materials also increased in the Gambia.

The pattern for trade for all European states was dictated by mercantilism. Companies would be formed by stockholders who would receive a charter from a European monarch giving them sole privileges to trade in a specific area. These companies would then attempt to exploit their grant by sending out to West Africa a wide variety of trade products to exchange for African goods. In some areas the company men would be forced to trade directly from their ships; in others they would be allowed by the African rulers to build temporary trading stations, and in a few instances, such as along the Gold Coast, the Europeans manned a series of permanent fortified trading posts.

Although British trade in the Senegambia dates to 1553

and the French to 1560, the first permanent station in the
Gambia was erected by citizens of the tiny Baltic principality
of Courland in 1651.   They purchased an island in the Gambia
River which they named St. Andrew's Island and there constructed a fort.   After a very brief interlude, the Courlanders were driven out by the English in 1661 who renamed the
tiny island after James, Duke of York.   James Island continued to be the center of English trading activities in the Gambia for over a century, first by the Royal Adventures Trading
in Africa, then the Royal African Company, and lastly by independent merchants.

French companies meanwhile had carved out a trading
sphere further to the north, at the mouth of the Senegal
River, and also opposite Cape Verde.   St. Louis was founded
in 1638, the island of Goree was taken from the Dutch in
1677, and the French established a station at Albreda opposite James Island in 1681.   The 18th-century history of the
French in the Senegambia is one of continual conflict with
British elements on the Gambia River.   For a brief period
after 1760, the British controlled all French territory and
created the Province of the Senegambia, only to return it all
to France after the Treaty of Versailles in 1783.   During the
last stages of the American Revolution, a French combined
force so completely destroyed the fort on James Island that
it was never occupied again.   British presence on the Gambia River in the last two decades of the 18th century was
maintained by private traders without any definite official support for their activities.

All was changed by the British decision to abolish the
slave trade as of January 1, 1808.   It then became necessary
to attempt to control the activities of British nationals along
the western coast of Africa.   For this purpose a part of the
British navy was delegated to patrol the coastline.   The force
needed harbor facilities and this involved the British government directly in the administration of the Freetown Colony,
and in 1816, Captain Alexander Grant was authorized to establish a base on the Gambia River.   He rejected the old
site of British authority, James Island, and instead negotiated the cession, by the king of Kombo, of St. Mary's Island,
adjacent to the south bank near the mouth of the river.   In
the next four years, Grant and his small garrison of a few
hundred troops constructed administration buildings, harbor
facilities; and barracks on the island.   Within months of its
beginning, the new town of Bathurst (today Banjul) had at-
tracted a considerable settlement of neighboring Africans.

In the 1820s and 1830s, the population of the area was greatly augmented by Wolof merchants from the Cape Verde area
and by Africans liberated from captured slave ships.  In 1821,
the administration of the new Colony was taken from the Company of Merchants and vested in the Governor of Freetown.
Affairs in the Gambia were handled directly by an Administrator subordinate to the Governor.  The size of the Colony
was increased in 1823 by the acquisition of MacCarthy Island
and in 1826 with the cession, by the ruler of Barra, of the
so-called Ceded Mile.

European trade rivalry and the change in the fortunes
of one state or another had little to do with the lives of the
majority of Africans in the Senegambia.  They, of course,
were affected by the volume, type, and direction of trade,
but direct relations with Europeans was not typical in the
Gambia.  Economic changes in all the kingdoms were not
revolutionary since the area never was a center for the slave
trade and there were few other products which the Europeans
wanted.  Thus the Mandingo polities along the river and the
Serer and Wolof states to the north continued to evolve slowly
with little outside interference.

In the early 19th century, there were nine Mandingo
kingdoms on the south side of the Gambia River--Kombo,
Foni, Kiang, Jarra, Niamina, Eropina, Jimara, Tomani, and
Kantora.  Along the north bank there were five kingdoms--
Niumi, Baddibu, Upper and Lower Niami, and Wuli.  Although each state was separate, and customs and politics differed to a certain extent in each, all of them shared certain
commonalities.  Each society was divided into three endoga-
mous castes--the freeborn, the artisans and praise singers,
and the slaves.  Each state had a king (mansa) chosen from
a specific royal lineage.  Each king had his council of advisors and an armed force to defend the state and with which,
if necessary, he could impose his will upon the state.  Each
kingdom was subdivided into territorial units of the village,
ward, and family compound.  Each village area was governed'
by a satiyo-tiyo, a representative of the senior lineage of the
village, and his council.  The ward leaders, or kabilo-tiyos,
administered their areas with the help of advisors.  Thus
each state was held together by a combination of tradition,
kinship patterns, and force.  The population of many of these
kingdoms was relatively homogeneous, but some of the kings
ruled over large non-Mandingo minorities.  There were Wolof
and Serer in Niumi and Baddibu, the Jola were located in
Kombo and Foni, and there were many Serahuli in the upriver

kingdom of Wuli. Large numbers of Fulbe had traditionally migrated from the Futa Toro to the Futa Jallon through some of the Mandingo states. By the mid-19th century the Fulbe had become a significant factor in the affairs of Eropina, Jimara, Tomani, and Kantora.

To the north of the Gambia River were the larger, more powerful polities of the Serer and Wolof. Each of the Wolof states had evolved from the earlier kingdom of Jolof. The Serer kingdoms of Sine and Saloum had evolved in the same period with a mixed population. The Wolof and Serer states, as the Mandingo, were of the Sudanic type with a king representing a particular lineage, nobles who controlled much of the land and who made up the king's councils and command-ed the armies, and peasants, artisans, and slaves. Each polity maintained a large army and there was incessant diplo-matic maneuvering and open warfare between the states be-cause each king was jealous of his prerogatives and wanted to dominate his neighbors.

In the 19th century all of the Senegambian kingdoms were subjected to new pressures and the intensification of old cleavages. After mid-century, the French became much more active in the hinterlands of the Senegambia. The for-ward policy of Governor Faidherbe converted much of the coastal region of Senegal into a practical French protectorate. Peanuts had become an important item of trade, particularly in Sine and Saloum, and French traders there demanded pro-tection. Attempts to provide this embroiled the French in the internal affairs of all the kingdoms north of the Gambia. The British government, although disavowing territorial ambi-tions, nevertheless interferred continually in the affairs of the Gambian kingdoms. From their base at Bathurst they mounted a number of punitive expeditions against both the traditional rulers and their Marabout challengers.

The most fundamental changes in the 19th century were introduced by proselytizing Muslim teachers. Islam had made slow but steady progress among the peoples of the Senegambia during the previous two centuries. The religious revival which had wrought such great reforms in the societies of Fu-ta Toro, Macina, Futa Jallon, and northern Nigeria reached the Senegambia by the 1850s. Seeking basic religious, social, and political reforms, the Marabouts and the growing number of their followers attacked the traditional Mandingo systems of rule in the kingdoms of the Gambia. Thus began the half-century of internecine conflicts known as the Soninke-Marabout Wars.

The first major test between the old order and the new religious beliefs occurred in the south bank kingdoms of Kombo and Foni. In Kombo, Fodi Kabba of Gunjur, operating with the followers of Omar of Sabaji from 1853 to 1855, conquered a large portion of the western section of the kingdom. When the British Administrator, Colonel O'Connor, appeared to favor the Soninke rulers, the Marabouts began planning for the total negation of British power. In June 1855, the Marabouts attacked the advanced elements of the British garrison and O'Connor and the bulk of his troops fell into a trap laid by the Marabouts. After sustaining casualties of over one-quarter of his force, the Administrator retreated to Bathurst. Only with extreme difficulty and considerable reinforcements was he able to defeat the Marabouts. Although O'Connor's final victory stabilized the British position, it ultimately did little to protect the traditional rulers, as yet more people pledged their loyalties to Fodi Kabba, Fodi Silla, and their lieutenants. The British would give no physical support to the traditional rulers, contenting themselves with intervening from time to time to arrange a truce between the protagonists. The last of these interludes in open warfare lasted for seven years after the truce of 1864. The final test of strength of the two factions in Kombo occurred between 1871-75. In the latter year, the king, Tomani Bojang, surrendered his last fortified town, accepted the peace terms of Fodi Silla, and became a Muslim.

During the decade of the 1860s, Fodi Kabba shifted the area of his activities to Foni and Kiang. Except in Jola country, he and the other Marabouts were generally successful in imposing their will upon the people. The Jola, however, remained stubbornly independent and "pagan." Fodi Kabba's forces did not receive a serious check in the other portions of these south bank kingdoms until they encountered the westward moving elements of the Fulbe armies loyal to Alfa and Musa Molloh. Eastern Kiang and western Jarra became for the rest of the century the rough dividing line between the territories controlled by Fodi Kabba and those by his enemies, the Mollohs.

The reforms demanded by the early Marabouts related specifically to the spread of Islam. They wanted to eradicate "pagan" influences and substitute for them a well ordered Muslim society. However, even at the beginning the movement drew to it a wide spectrum of protestors, many of whom were little concerned with the advancement of Islam. Throughout the Gambia the initial Marabout successes were tied to the

military or political skill of a few men.  As these men supplanted their Soninke enemies, they tended to lose their religious fervor and much of- the warfare after 1870 was motivated primarily by personal or economic considerations with
religion having little causative effect.  Although this shift of
emphasis is quite noticeable in the careers of Fodi Kabba
and Fodi Silla, the best illustration of the secular nature of
revolt against traditional authority is the career of the Mollohs in their state of Fuladu.

   During the first half of the 19th century, there was an
increasing influx of Fulbe into the south bank kingdoms of
Tomani, Jimara, and Eropina.  A Fulbe elephant hunter of
Jimara who later took the name Alfa Molloh and was re-
nowned for his ability with arms, quarrelled with his Mandingo overlord in the late 1860s.   This began a revolt which,
within five years, swept away the old system of government.
In this phase as well as in later wars, Alfa Molloh counted
heavily on the support of his fellow Fulbe rulers in the
theocracies of Futa Toro and the Futa Jallon.   It was believed that he had taken the Tijaniyya oath and had been created a deputy of Al Hajj Umar.   Such rumors did not damage
his image and were important in gaining Muslim adherents.
However, the mantle of religious reformer rested lightly upon
Alfa, and his son, Musa, was even less committed to the
spread of Islam.   They ranged themselves against Fodi Kabba,
and in the 1880s, Musa consistently allied his state against
the expansion of Ma Bâ's successors.   Both the Mollohs were
more concerned with the preservation of Fuladu, which they
had created, than with advancing the cause of their religion
against traditional "pagan" beliefs.

   After Alfa's death in 1881, Fuladu was divided into
two segments since by the Fulbe law of succession, the kingship was inherited by Musa's uncle, Bakari Dembel.   Musa,
who had led his father's armies, refused to accept completely
this deposition and led his followers southward and established
a fortified base in Hamdallai.   He continued to pay nominal
allegiance to his uncle, but it was Musa who was the real
power in Fuladu.   Finally in 1892, he moved against Bakari
and proclaimed himself king of Fuladu.   Long before this,
Musa had created the best organized state in the Gambia.
The highly centralized bureaucracy of the state placed almost
absolute civil power in his hands.   His control of the military forces assured Musa that his authority over his section
of Fuladu was complete.   This Fulbe autocracy would be al-
tered only by the actions of the French and British.

The only serious attempt during the Soninke-Marabout Wars to establish a true theocracy of the type successfully achieved by Al Hajj Umar and Usuman dan Fodio was that of Ma Bâ, the ruler of Baddibu.   Ma Bâ, a religious teacher, puritan, and Tijaniyya reformer, seized power in Baddibu in 1861, driving out the traditional rulers.   Very soon he had gathered around him a significant number of believers, and with this force, attempted first to expand his control over Niumi.   Here he encountered active opposition from the British and personally abandoned the forceful incorporation of that state into his kingdom.   However, his lieutenant, Amer Faal, continued the Marabout conquests there, and by the 1880s, the bulk of Niumi was controlled by the Muslims.

Ma Bâ differed from most of his contemporary rulers because he envisioned himself always as the religious teacher and leader who was merely working out God's will in destroying the pagan kimgdoms of the Senegambia.   His armies were led by subordinates.   Only once did his forces seriously attempt to gain a foothold on the south bank.   In 1863, Ma Bâ authorized a large segment of his army to cross the river and attack the Soninkes in Kiang.   In one of the major battles of the Soninke-Marabout Wars, Ma Bâ's forces were decisively beaten at Quinella.   After this, Ma Bâ turned his full attention toward the overthrow of the Serer and Wolof states to the north.

In his attempt to create a large Senegambian theocracy, Ma Bâ was aided by the ex-rulers of Cayor, Macadou and Lat Dior, and their followers.   By early 1865, the bulk of Saloum was under his control and that summer his forces conquered Jolof.   At this juncture his schemes were foiled by the French.   They had at first welcomed Ma Bâ since it appeared that he was weakening the power of the traditional rulers in Senegal.   However, he had succeeded too well. The French, who considered the entire Senegal as a trading sphere, did not want a large powerful unified polity to take the place of the divided, weaker traditional states.   Governor Pinet-Laprade of Senegal decided to halt Ma Bâ's advance and proceeded to Kaolack with approximately five thousand men.   At the battle of Pathebadiane in November 1865, the French and their allies were narrowly defeated and forced to retreat.   Ma Bâ, however, was attempting too much with his limited forces.   He was supporting Lat Dior in southern Cayor and Amer Faal in Niumi as well as maintaining forces in Saloum and Jolof.   In 1867, Ma Bâ decided to end the potential threat of the Serer state of Sine and accompanied his

army in its invasion.  In the most crucial conflict of the
Soninke-Marabout Wars, the Sine forces defeated those of Ma
Bâ and the prophet teacher himself was killed.

The practical realization of the dream of a united
Senegambia ended with Ma Bâ's death.  Within a brief period,
Saloum and Jolof became independent and Baddibu itself was
rent by civil war.  The chiefs of Baddibu selected Ma Bâ's
brother, Mamadou N'Dare, as the ruler, but within a decade
his rule was disputed by one of his lieutenants, Biram Cisse.
Soon afterward, Ma Bâ's son, Saër Maty, also claimed the
throne.  In the armed conflicts which followed, Mamadou lost
most of his power and the kimgdom was ruled by Biram
Cisse and Saër Maty.  This state of affairs reduced Baddibu's
power to a mere cipher and made its absorption by the French
and British easy.

The continuing disturbances of the Soninke-Marabout
Wars interfered with trade and made the British possessions
on the Gambia River appear worthless to a Parliament and
Ministry devoted to saving money.  All the Administrators of
the Gambia were under orders to do nothing which would in-
volve the British in a major conflict in the hinterland.  Thus
they acted against the Soninkes or Marabouts only when it
was impossible to avoid some kind of definite action and when
the chances of precipitating a larger conflict appeared minimal.  Otherwise, the British were content to act as arbiters
in the conflicts.  The Parliamentary Report of 1865 confirmed
the no-expansion policy in the Gambia.

The French, however, since the governorship of Faidherbe, had been pursuing an aggressive trade policy in the
independent Wolof and Serer states.  The increasing value of
the peanut crop aided the few, but ardent, French imperial-
ists in Senegal and in France.  These men saw a potentially
great future for France in West Africa.  Thus the governors
of Senegal used what military forces they had to upset Wolof
governments in Baol, Walo, and Cayor in order to blunt the
westward ambitions of Al Hajj Umar and his son, Ahmadu,
to build forts in Sine, Saloum, and Jolof, and to help defeat
Ma Bâ's ambitions.

It is not surprising, therefore, that the French government should approach the British concerning an exchange of
some French territory in return for the British possession
on the Gambia River.  The idea of such a trade was first
suggested by the French in 1866.  After four years of nego-

tiations, almost all the details for an exchange had been completed when the onset of the Franco-Prussian War stopped
all discussions.    Internal difficulties in France postponed the
resumption of negotiations until 1875.    The French Foreign
Ministry again found the British government receptive to their
proposals.    However, a combination of Parliamentary and
commercial opposition from British and Gambian merchants
halted the exchange.    Despite this failure, the French government was convinced that, in time, Britain would cede the unwanted territory and France would be in possession of the
Gambia River, the most economical highway to the interior
of West Africa.

The "scramble" for Africa became a reality in the
decade of the 1880s and the French began to occupy coastal
areas which had long been considered British spheres.    In
Senegal they absorbed the coastal Wolof states and began in
the late 1880s to interfere in the quarrels in Baddibu and
Fuladu.    The British government, spurred on by the urgings
of the Gambian Administrators who believed that Britain was
about to lose the Gambia by default, finally authorized the
establishment of a Protectorate.    In 1888, the Gambia was
separated from the administrative control of Sierra Leone.
In the following year, British and French representatives met
in Paris to allocate spheres of influence in West Africa.
The British delegation was prepared to cede the Gambia provided the French would be more flexible in their demands
elsewhere.    When it became apparent that the French delegates were not prepared to compromise, the British demanded
control of the river.    British lack of interest in territorial
acquisition in the Senegambia can be seen by their refusal to
demand more territory than that represented by the narrow
riverine strip which the French were willing to admit was a
British sphere.    However, neither power considered that the
boundaries drawn by the Anglo-French Convention of 1889
were to be permanent.

Administrator Llewellyn had seen British policy change
in the space of a few months from non-expansionist to expansionist.    After the 1889 Convention he was charged with developing some suitable method of bringing law and order to
the new Protectorate and devising a permanent system of
government for the area.    At first he could do little but announce the Protectorate and enter into generalized agreements
with various Gambian chiefs.    His first use of the military
was in 1891 to protect the Anglo-French Boundary Commissioners from possible attack by Fodi Kabba and Fodi Silla.

Later in January 1893, he assigned two Travelling Commissioners, one for the north bank and another for the south, to
convey his orders and requests to the Gambian rulers.   In
the following year the government issued the first comprehensive Protectorate Ordinance.   Although the full implications
of this ordinance were not felt for some time,  it established
the form of government for the bulk of the Gambia which was
to continue until just prior to independence.   Later called
"indirect rule, " this sytem had the advantage of disturbing
the Protectorate Gambians the least,  and yet the British authorities at Bathurst could control overall political activities
in the Protectorate by ordinances which were then enforced
by their Commissioners.

The British and French Convention of 1889 in the
Senegambia presented many of the Gambian rulers with almost insoluble problems.   The accord meant for some the
division of their kingdoms, forcing them to make a choice of
which European government to accept as their overlord.   To
others,  the establishment of European authority meant the
abandonment of a life style which had been established for
over a generation.   Fodi Silla was the first to feel the changed
nature of European activity.   After he had been overawed by
British gunboats in 1891,  he remained quiescent until 1893,
recognized by the British as the ruler of western Kombo.
Then problems related to trade, particularly his participation
in the slave trade, decided the British to invade his territory.
In February 1894, his main base of Gunjur was taken and he
was forced to flee to the Casamance.   There he was arrested
by French authorities and deported to St. Louis.

Fodi Kabba in 1892 retired to the Casamance where he
continued to support those Gambians dissatisfied with British
rule.   Periodically his followers would go on raids into the
Gambia and retreat to French territory before effective pursuit could be organized.   In 1900, at Sankandi, Travelling
Commissioner Sitwell and other members of his party were
killed.   The town was known to be allied to Fodi Kabba, and
the British and French subsequently decided to end his power
permanently.   A joint military venture was mounted in 1901,
and in March of that year Fodi Kabba was killed.

Musa Molloh of Fuladu had decided in the early 1890s
to live in peace with his neighbors and the Europeans.   He
chose to continue to live at Hamdallai in the Casamance and
cooperated with the French.   In 1901, he took part in the
expedition against his old enemy, Fodi Kabba.   However, his

freedom from direct control had passed, and when the French
decided to build a military post at Hamdallai, he burned the
town and retreated with many of his followers to British
Fuladu.   There he was recognized as chief, received a stipend, and was generally left alone until after World War I.
Then, reacting to rumors of his cruel and arbitrary actions,
the British deposed him and sent him into exile.   Four years
later, in 1923, he was allowed to return, but was almost
completely stripped of power in the small territory which the
British alloted to him.

British assumption of power in the Gambia was largely
without incident.   Most Gambians were obviously exhausted by
the half-century of wars and many welcomed peace.   The
system of "indirect rule" as developed in the 20th century
left almost unchanged the political and social systems which
had existed prior to 1889.   During the first 35 years of the
20th century, there were enacted a series of Protectorate
Ordinances which fixed the responsibilities of the state supported chiefs, the District Officers, and the central administration.   In very general terms, the central government,
which was also that of the Colony area, comprised the Governor, the appointive Legislative and Executive Councils, the
Secretariat, and the various departments such as Agriculture,
Marine, and Public Works.   The central government made
all laws and regulations for the Protectorate and the departments were responsible for work undertaken in the areas of
their jurisdiction in the Protectorate.   Government in the
Protectorate was carried on by a minimal number of District
Officers who supervised the work of the 35 recognized chiefs
and who saw that the laws passed by the central government
were carried out.

The key to social and economic development of the
British system of rule in all Africa was the amount of money
the Treasury would appropriate.   The British Colonial Office
followed a general rule that all territories had to live within
their budgets.   This meant that more economically viable territories such as Nigeria could expect considerable development of roads, transport, agriculture, and even education.
A small, poor area such as the Gambia was hard pressed
just to meet its recurrent budget.   Another facet of British
financial administration was its conservatism.   Although the
Gambia had acquired considerable cash reserves by 1918,
these funds normally were not used for development.   Thus
few improvements were made in the Protectorate until after
World War II when Colonial Development and Welfare funds

became available for the first time.    The Colony areas were
more fortunate.    In Bathurst, the port facilities were improved, some streets were paved, there was a hospital, and
the missionary groups maintained elementary and secondary
schools there.

       The Gambia in the first half of the 20th century had
progressed very little.    It was sustained by a single export
crop, peanuts, whose taxable value was just enough to keep
the government functioning.    Beginning in 1942, the British
government held out for the Gambia promises of a better future when Colonial Development and Welfare funds would become available.    These promises were never fully realized,
although some of the funds appropriated allowed for improvements in the water supply, streets, and harbor facilities of
the capital city.    By 1947, it was apparent that the moneys
promised for improving Bathurst, building a new government
center, and modernizing the airport would not be forthcoming.
The British government decision not to improve Yundum airport meant that the worldwide air transport system would not
have a major base in the Gambia.    The major airlines instead chose Dakar where the French were more willing to
invest in the necessary facilities.    The Colonial Development
Corporation wasted over £2 million between 1947-1951 in
two schemes--the Yundum Egg Project and the Rice Farm
at Wallikunda.    Each of these failed more because of administrative error than any other factor.    Nevertheless, the
failures inhibited any further major development projects by
the British for the Gambia.    Thus in the 1950s, the Gambia
was still dependent upon one crop, and its communications
and transport infrastructure were still primitive.    In the
Protectorate there were no all-weather roads, only one secondary school, and one hospital for over a quarter of a million people.

       The post-World War II years elsewhere in British
Africa witnessed the rise of nationalistic movements which
sought greater African participation in government.    This
nationalism, combined with the desire of the British government to be rid of non-profitable areas, wrought a revolution
in Africa within a decade.    The British began by making
concessions to the Western educated, middle-class Africans,
recognized African political parties, and eventually negotiated
for the independence of their African territories.    In 1957,
Ghana became independent, in 1960 Nigeria, and in 1961
Sierra Leone, leaving the Gambia as the only area in West
Africa still under British control.    In the 1950s, there had

been some concessions which allowed more Gambian participation in the central government.    In 1947, 1952, and 1954,
there were changes in the size and composition of the Legislative and Executive Councils.    According to the provisions of
the 1954 Constitution, Gambians held 16 of the 21 positions
on the Legislative Council and there was a form of Ministerial government.    Nevertheless, the real power resided in the
Governor and the higher administrative officers, almost all
of whom were English expatriates.    The Protectorate government was still dominated by the District Officers and the
chiefs who were generally responsive to the wishes of the
Governor.    All Protectorate representatives to the Legislative Council were chosen by indirect election.

Political parties were formed very late in the Gambia
and they tended to reflect Colony interests and were normally
the vehicles by which one man could be elected to the Legislative Council.    John C. Faye was instrumental in creating
the Democratic Alliance in 1951, I. M. Garba-Jahumpa
formed the Muslim Congress later that same year, and in
1952 the supporters of P. S. N'Jie began the United Party.
These parties debated local Colony issues, and were prevented by law from campaigning in the Protectorate.

One of the major reasons for the lack of a national
policy was the confusion in almost every quarter about the
Gambia's future.    It appeared that the territory was too
small and poor to consider independence as a viable goal.
Before the time of the independence of other British West
African territories, there was some consideration given to a
federal arrangement with another area.    The Malta Plan was
also briefly considered as an alternative to direct control.
This envisioned a type of continuing political association between small, economically insecure parts of the Empire and
the British Parliament.    After Malta opted for independence,
any hope that this scheme would work was given up.

The devolution of power to Africans in British territories represented a reversal of a philosophy of government
which had been dominant throughout the century.    If any of
the new African states were to have a chance of economic
and political stability without serious alterations of its boundaries and general system of government, they had to be
ruled by Western educated men.    Very few traditional rulers
had any type of Western education.    Furthermore, indirect
rule was fundamentally divisive.    Therefore, it could not be
used as a means of achieving national unity.    It is ironic

that in the decade of the 1950s, the British government
turned over their rule to a group they had previously suspected and even disliked--the educated minority.   In the Gambia this process was particularly difficult for the Colonial
Office since they had always supported the chiefs in governing the Protectorate.   Educated, Colony-based Gambians had
been specifically prohibited from any type of political activity
in the Protectorate.   However, with the grant of independence
to other West African territories, the British could not re-
fuse the demands of Gambian political parties that the elective principle be extended to the Protectorate.   The Constitution of 1960 provided for direct elections for the seven
Colony and 12 Protectorate seats in the House.   The chiefs'
powers to influence central policy were minimized since they
had the right to select only eight members of the Legislature.

A new political party, the Protectorate People's Party,
was formed in 1959 by a Protectorate veterinary officer,
David Jawara, and his associates.   This party appealed most
directly to the Protectorate since its leaders were primarily
Mandingo and they stressed how much the Protectorate had
been ignored in the past.   The United Party, led by P. S.
N'Jie, also expected to do well in the elections of 1960.
N'Jie had gained a considerable reputation in the 1950s as
an opponent of the policies of the British dominated government.   The leaders of the other major parties, I. M. Garba-
Jahumpa and John C. Faye, joined their two parties together
just before the election to form the Democratic Congress Alliance.   All parties campaigned vigorously throughout the
Protectorate, and despite the newness of the elective principle,
there was very heavy voter participation in the elections of
1960.

Due to the nature of the Constitution, the elections produced a veritable stalemate.   Jawara's party, now renamed
the People's Progressive Party, won eight Protectorate seats,
the United Party gained five Colony and one Protectorate seat,
and the Democratic Congress Alliance won only three seats.
The eight chiefs selected in an indirect fashion thus became
very important, not only for the composition of the House and
in selecting the Ministers, but for the appointment of a Chief
Minister.   Late in 1960, the Governor had indicated that he
would appoint such an official.   Since the chiefs would not
support Jawara and the P. P. P. refused to sanction a chief
to hold this position, the Governor appointed P. S. N'Jie of
the United Party as the Gambia's first Chief Minister.   Jawara and the other P. P. P. ministers immediately resigned
from the government.

It was very soon apparent that the 1960 Constitution was not satisfactory to any of the Gambian factions. Two Constitutional Conferences were held in May and July 1961, resulting in a new instrument which provided for responsible government. The British in the new Constitution finally abandoned support of the Protectorate chiefs. Thus in the 36-man House, the chiefs had only four indirectly elected representatives while 25 members were to be directly elected from the Protectorate. New elections were held in 1962, and the results were a vindication of the claim of the People's Progressive Party that the previous government was not representative. They gained over 64 per cent of all votes cast and won 18 seats, while the United Party could gain but 13. David Jawara became the Prime Minister, and the People's Progressive Party exclusively formed the executive. Even before the election of 1962, it was apparent that within a short period the Gambia would receive its independence, although there still existed serious doubts in Britain about the ability of the area to afford that status. In 1963, the Gambia received the grant of full self-government, and discussions were soon begun on the mechanisms of independence and the date for this goal. Despite protests from the United Party, the British government agreed with Jawara that there was no need for new elections before the grant of independence. On February 18, 1965, the Gambia became an independent nation within the Commonwealth. Only four years had elapsed since the Governor had agonized over the decision to appoint a Chief Minister with very circumscribed powers.

It is no exaggeration to say that independent Gambia has been an unexpected success story. The People's Progressive Party government very early decided to live within the limited financial resources of the country. It maintains diplomatic relations with only Senegal, Britain, and the United Nations. The salaries of ministers and members of the House of Representatives are among the lowest in Africa. The development programs, although providing for the all-weather trans-Gambian road, improved river transport, and considerable progress in rice cultivation, have been modest. The moderate economic policies of the government of Sir Dauda Jawara (he changed his name and was knighted in 1966), combined with an improvement in the price of peanuts, enabled it to dispense with British grants-in-aid for the recurrent budget. The Gambia is one of the few states in Africa which has remained faithful to the basic concepts of democratic government. Although the potential of the opposition parties has declined drastically in the past decade, there has been no move by the government to restrict criticism or to create a one-party state.

There is no better illustration of the Gambia's adherence to majority rule than the Republic issue. Very soon after independence, Premier Jawara became convinced that the Westminster form of government placed him, as the practical ruler of the state, at a disadvantage in dealing with other African leaders. The People's Progressive Party began a campaign to convince Gambians that a Presidential form would solve this problem and give the Gambia a stronger government. When a plebiscite on this question was submitted to the voters in November 1965, they rejected the proposal by approximately 800 votes, and the government bowed to their wishes. The question was not resubmitted to the voters until 1970, and this time it was approved. The Gambia then became a Republic on April 24, 1970, and Sir Dauda became its first President.

Another crucial problem which faced the government during the decade of the 1960s concerned closer association with Senegal. Many observers had considered some form of political association inevitable. Senegal, surrounding the tiny enclave, was larger, more economically advanced, and was composed of the same national groupings as represented in the Gambia. P. S. N'Jie and President Senghor in 1961 created the first inter-Ministerial committee to consult on problems connected with rapprochement. A United Nations Committee reported on the economic advantages in terms that indicated that in time such a political association was a foregone conclusion. However, the problems of language, law, education, and differential Western administration and customs could not be ignored. Neither could the substantial fears of Gambians that their interests would be submerged in any political association. Although much discussion has taken place and some economic and cultural agreements have been made, a permanent political association seems further away than in 1965. Part of the reason for this relates to the improved economic position of the Gambia, while that of Senegal has declined. The decade of self-rule under a responsible government has convinced many Gambians, who earlier had thought otherwise, that they could govern themselves, and therefore no particular advantage could be gained by a merger with Senegal.

However improbable the state of the Gambia might have seemed to some in 1965, it has shown a political ma-

turity unmatched by most other African states.   Although
prognostication concerning the future of any African polity is
risky,  it does appear that this area,  demarcated almost as
an afterthought by two European powers in 1889,  has an excellent chance of survival.

# ABBREVIATIONS

| | |
|---|---|
| CD&W | Colonial Development and Welfare |
| CDC | Colonial Development Corporation |
| DCA | Democratic Congress Alliance |
| DP | Democratic Party |
| GNP | Gambia National Party |
| GNU | Gambia National Union |
| GWU | Gambia Workers Union |
| GOMB | Groundnut Oilseeds Marketing Board |
| MCP | Muslim Congress Party |
| PPA | People's Progressive Alliance |
| PPP | People's Progressive Party (originally Protectorate People's Party) |
| RAC | Royal African Corps |
| UP | United Party |
| WAFF | West Africa Field Force |

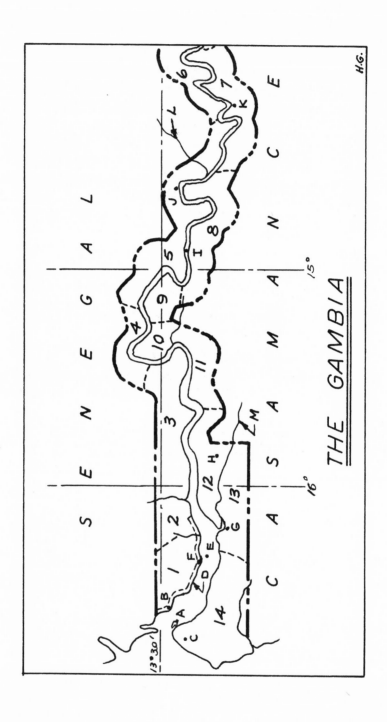

THE GAMBIA

## MAP KEY

### Nineteenth Century States

| | | | |
|---|---|---|---|
| 1. | Niumi | 8. | Jimara |
| 2. | Jokadu | 9. | Eropina |
| 3. | Baddibu | 10. | Niamina |
| 4. | Saloum | 11. | Jarra |
| 5. | Niani | 12. | Kiang |
| 6. | Wuli | 13. | Foni |
| 7. | Tomani | 14. | Kombo |

### Towns and Other Sites

| | | | |
|---|---|---|---|
| A. | St. Marys Island, & Banjul (Bathurst) | H. | Sankandi |
| | | I. | MacCarthy Island & Georgetown |
| B. | Ft. Bullen | | |
| C. | Sukuta (Sabaji) | J. | Karantaba (Pisania) |
| D. | The Ceded Mile | K. | Basse |
| E. | James Island | L. | Sami Creek (Bolon) |
| F. | Albreda | M. | Bintang Creek |
| G. | Bentang | | |

# THE DICTIONARY

AHMADIYYA. A Pakistan-based sect of Islam created in the 19th century by Hazrat Mirza Ahmad. Its major theme is the reconciliation of Islam and Christianity. In the last four decades, active proselytizing by missionary teachers has converted many Africans, particularly in coastal towns, to this belief.

AKU. A title given to the Yoruba recaptives. It has been misused by some observers to mean all the recaptives' Westernized descendants and non-Gambian African residents in the Colony areas. In the Gambia, the Aku in the late 19th and 20th centuries came to exercise an influence far beyond their numbers. They adopted Western modes of living, accepted Christianity, and educated their children in Sierra Leone and Great Britain. The Aku became successful traders, entered the civil service, and in the period between 1945 and independence came to dominate many of the important government positions in the Gambia.

ALBREDA. Today a small river-port village located in upper Niumi. It was for a long time the trading center for the French in their efforts to dominate the Gambia River trade. The French Senegal Company first obtained trading rights to that portion of the north bank area in 1679, and Albreda was established two years later opposite the English station on James Island. During the century-long period of wars between England and France, Albreda was looted and abandoned many times. The French retained their proprietary rights to the area until the Convention of 1857 with Britain gave them exclusive rights to Portendic in return for relinquishing their claims to Albreda.

ALKALI. A title given to an African ruler's representative to a European trading area. In time, it came to mean to the Mandingo the same as satiyo-tiyo or a village head.

23

ALMAMY. The spiritual leader in Muslim societies who was concerned with prayer, education, and general religious rule making. In many Mandingo villages there was a type of dual control between the religious leader and the alkali, the secular leader.

AMER FAAL. One of the chief lieutenants of Ma Bâ in the Kombo and Ceded Mile areas between 1864-66. The difficulties there were precipitated by the British decision to allow refugees from the wars in Saloum to settle in the Ceded Mile area. In 1866, Amer Faal's continual raids reopened the question of British supremacy along the lower north bank territory. In 1866, a large mixed British expedition was mounted against Amer Faal and the Marabouts. Albreda was taken without casualties, but Amer Faal's main stockaded base, Tubab Kolon, was taken by storm.

ANGLO-FRENCH CONVENTION, 1882. The culmination of over three years effort by the British Foreign Office which wanted a clear demarcation of British and French spheres of influence in West Africa. The Convention granted most of the French claims along the coast between Conakry and Freetown, and called for both Britain and France to maintain the status quo. Implicit in the Convention was the desire to rectify spheres of influence, and this very clearly meant an exchange of the Gambia for some suitable territory elsewhere. Although the British Foreign Office continued for some time to recognize the status quo, the Convention never became effective because the French Chamber of Deputies refused to ratify the agreement.

ANGLO-FRENCH CONVENTION, 1889. The result of British pressures begun in 1887 to have a specific understanding with the French government on delimitation of territory in Senegambia. By the close of 1888, the French were present in a number of places along the banks of the Gambia River, and British authorities in the Gambia had begun to collect treaties with riverine rulers. In April 1889, a high level series of meetings began in Paris with the object of warding off any possible conflict between the agents of the two powers in the Gambia, Sierra Leone, Ghana, and Nigeria. The Convention as signed did establish coastal boundary lines between the spheres of influence of the two powers in all of these areas, but the agreement had more far-reaching

ramifications for the Gambia than for any of the other
areas in western Africa.   E. H. Egerton of the Foreign
Office and Augustus Hemming of the Colonial Office
represented Britain while the French delegates were M.
Nisard, Director of Protectorates of the Foreign Ministry, and M. Bayol, Governor of Senegal.   The British
delegates at first tried to obtain a clear cut demarcation of spheres of influence in western Africa.   Failing
in this, they decided to force the French to recognize
their claims to both banks of the Gambia River and thus
they conceded the hinterland of the Gambia to French
control.   At the third general session, this limited
British objective was gained when the French delegates
admitted in principle that the Gambia was a British
river.   M. Bayol drew two lines upon a map from the
mouth of the river to Yarbutenda and stated that within
these lines was the territory that could be reasonably
assigned to Britain.   Ultimately the two parties agreed
on British occupation rights to the banks of the Gambia
ten kilometers north and south of the river as far inland as Yarbutenda and there the eastern boundary of
the Gambia was to end on a ten kilometer radius drawn
from the center of the town.   Both the French and the
British negotiators considered the agreements reached
regarding the boundaries of the Gambia to be only temporary.   The British believed that in the future they
would be able to trade their exclusive rights to the down
river areas for concessions by the French elsewhere in
Africa or in the world.   The French believed that in
time the British government would realize the non-viable character of their new Protectorate and would be
more than willing to allow it to be absorbed by Senegal.
Neither of these prognoses proved to be correct.   The
decade following the Anglo-French Convention of 1904
saw both governments unwilling to test the new found
entente by raising embarrassing questions about an area
which neither party considered to be very important.
Thus the boundary agreed upon in 1889 and demarcated
on the ground in the 1890s became the permanent boundary between the Gambia and Senegal.

ANGLO-FRENCH CONVENTION, 1904.   This most important
    agreement cleared the way for the entente between
    France and Britain which was to have such fateful con-
    sequences for European peace in the summer of 1914.
    The agreement finally settled the most outstanding dif-
    ferences between the two states regarding fishing rights

off Newfoundland, spheres of influence in northern
Africa, and border disputes in western and central
Africa.   Article five of the agreement ceded Yarbuten-
da to France with the stipulation that if the Gambia
River was not navigable for sea-going vessels at that
point, then the French would be given access to terri-
tory lower down on the Gambia River.   Although the
Convention was very explicit on this point, the British
Foreign Office later resisted the claims made by the
French for such mid-river enclaves.   The excuse of the
British for delaying action on the French demands for
a river port was that such an enclave would allow the
French to draw off the bulk of the peanut exports and
thus Bathurst and the British Protectorate would be
even more poverty stricken than was then the case.
Although the French government in the period from 1906
to 1910 were very active in pressing for the mid-river
port and some of their officials in Senegal revived the
plans for an exchange of territories, they were very
careful not to allow this question to endanger the new
found but shaky friendship between Britain and France.
The thrust of French policy in the early part of the
20th century was to gain support for what they considered to be their inevitable confrontation with Germany
in Europe.   After 1910, the French government ceased
to press Britain for territorial enclaves on the Gambia
or exchanges of territory.   The first World War and
the building of the railway and road system in Senegal,
and the concentration of French capital in the ports of
Kaolack and Ziganchour made the possession of the
Gambia less important to France.   After 1918, virtually
all diplomatic activity concerning an exchange of territory for the Gambia ceased.   Thus the boundaries established in 1889 which had been considered temporary
expedients became permanent political realities.

ANTONIO,  PRIOR OF CRATO.   In the period after 1580, one
of the claimants to the Portuguese throne.   Phillip II
of Spain, the champion of Catholicism and the enemy
of England, had in that year amalgamated the thrones
of Spain and Portugal.   The Prior, believing himself
to be the true king of Portugal, rented certain trading
concessions in Portuguese territory to English merchants.
It was on the basis of these concessions that Queen
Elizabeth in 1588 granted exclusive trading rights for
a period of ten years to certain English merchants trading in West Africa.   The company which was thus formed

was the first organized effort on the part of the English
to exploit the imagined wealth of western Africa.

ARCHER, FRANCIS BISSET.   Government official and author,
posted to the Gambia from Nigeria in January 1903, as
Colonial Treasurer.   He also served as acting Colonial
Secretary in 1904 and 1905, and briefly in 1905 was
the acting Governor of the Gambia.   In 1905, he authored the first book specifically devoted to the Gambia
entitled, The Gambia Colony and Protectorate:   An Official Handbook.

ARMITAGE, SIR C. H.   Governor of the Gambia from 1920
to 1927.   He was in charge of administration during
the recession following World War I and was partially
responsible for the slowness in recalling from circulation the French five franc piece.   This demonitization
crisis ultimately cost the Gambia over £200,000.   Governor Armitage's main positive contributions to the
Gambia were the establishment of the Agriculture Department in 1924 and the founding of a secondary school
for the sons of chiefs at Georgetown in 1923.

ARMITAGE SCHOOL.   Established by Governor Armitage at
Georgetown in 1923 as a school for the sons of chiefs.
Intended to give its students the rudiments of reading
and writing, it long catered to the Protectorate aris-
tocracy.   In the 1920s there were only two main elementary schools for the Protectorate.   One was a Catholic school at Basse, and the other a Wesleyan school
at Georgetown.   There was, therefore, little demand
for more secondary school facilities until after World
War II.   The expansion of all education in the postwar
years dictated improvements to Armitage.   It became
a boarding post-primary school, the only one in the
Protectorate.   In 1961 its facilities were expanded to
accommodate 200 pupils.

ASSOCIATION FOR THE DISCOVERY OF THE INTERIOR
REGIONS OF AFRICA.   An organization created in
1788 by Sir Joseph Banks and other Englishmen with
similar curiosity about the unexplored parts of the
world.   Of particular interest to the Association was
the question of the existence of the Niger River.   If it
existed, where was its source, in what direction did it
flow, was it connected with the Gambia, Senegal, and
Nile Rivers, and what was its outlet?   The Association

first sponsored two expeditions, one to cross the Sa-
hara from North Africa, and the other from Egypt.
Both ended in failure.  They next commissioned Major
Houghton who set out from the Gambia in November
1790, to penetrate the mysteries of the western Sudan.
He was killed after accomplishing little that he had expected to achieve.  The most successful venture sponsored by the Association was that of the young Scottish
physician, Mungo Park, who in December 1795 left the
upper river station of Pisania on the Gambia.  Park
eventually reached Segu on the Niger before being
forced to turn back.  His two and one-half year journey
was the first successful European exploration of the
interior of Africa and helped the Association convince
the British government to support further exploration.


-B-


BÂ, MA (also known as Amad Bâ or Maba).  The son of
    N'Dougou Pende Bâ, a Koranic teacher in a largely
    Wolof area of Baddibu.  Ma Bâ received Koranic edu-
    cation in Cayor, and then later taught the Koran in
    Jolof.  While in Jolof, Ma Bâ married the niece of the
    Burba Jolof and thus forged ties with the premier Wolof
    state.  After his father's death, Ma Bâ returned to
    Baddibu to assume his father's responsibilities.  Proba-
    bly in 1850, Ma Bâ had his only meeting with Al Hajj
    Umar at the village of Kabakoto, and at the conclusion
    of that meeting, Ma Bâ was chosen as the Tijaniyya
    representative in Baddibu.  During the decade of the
    1850s, Ma Bâ continued teaching the Koran in Baddibu.
    There is some confusion as to why he turned from such
    peaceful activities.  The most likely conclusion is that
    he, an Islamic teacher with considerable following
    among the people of Baddibu, was caught up in a clash
    between the Mandingo rulers and the British.  In 1861,
    the British decided to punish the king of Baddibu for
    his harassment of Bathurst traders.  Governor D'Arcy
    coordinated his offensive against Baddibu with the ef-
    forts of the French moving through Saloum, and the
    king of Baddibu was quickly defeated.  Presumably Ma
    Bâ had aided the British in the course of their invasion
    and had helped to arrange the peace terms.  After the
    war, the king of Baddibu decided to rid himself of this
    potential enemy with such a large Muslim following and
    sent his son to kill Ma Bâ.  Instead, the son was

killed by Ma Bâ's followers and the revolt in Baddibu
began.  Within a short period of time, the Marabout
forces had overcome their Mandingo overlords, the
king was killed, and large numbers of his followers
forced into exile.  The success of Ma Bâ's revolt
caused other Marabouts on the north bank to look to
him for aid, and in May 1862, Ma Bâ sent his army
into Niumi to aid his fellow Muslims.  An invasion of
Baddibu by the Bur Saloum forced Ma Bâ to retreat.
Later he recognized the independence of Niumi with the
stipulation that it pay him a tribute through his lieutenant, Amer Faal.  In the subsequent campaigning
against Saloum, Ma Bâ was generally successful so
that by the fall of 1863, the Marabout forces responsive to Ma Bâ controlled most of the territory between
the Gambia and the Saloum rivers except a part of
Niumi.  Ma Bâ's sphere of influence extended northward into eastern Saloum as far as Jolof.  Unlike many
of the other war chiefs or Marabouts of the Senegambia,
Ma Bâ was motivated primarily by the hope of creating
a large, viable Islamic state.  He was, like Usuman
dan Fodio and later Muhammad Ahmed, the director of
a religio-political movement rather than merely a war-
rior.  Ma Bâ's desires, however, ran counter to the
plans of the French who were concerned with dominating
the trade of the Serer states of Sine and Saloum.  The
anxiety of the French administrators and traders was
increased by the conversion of Macadou and Lat Dior,
both ex-damels of Cayor, who had been replaced by the
French because of their opposition toward French policies.  The French at first welcomed Ma Bâ's activities
since he was weakening the power of the Wolof and
Serer tyeddos.  In October 1865, the French by treaty
recognized Ma Bâ as the Almami of Baddibu and of
Saloum, and he agreed to respect the rights of French
traders already in Saloum.  In June 1865, Ma Bâ sent
his forces northward into Jolof and within a few months
he was in almost complete control of that Wolof state.
A revolt in Saloum forced him to devote his total attention again to the south and doomed his plans for a union
with the Trarza Moors to the north of the Senegal River.
In November 1865, the French governor, Pinet-Laprade,
disturbed over Ma Bâ's power and influence, led a
large army reported to be upwards of 5000 men overland to strike at Ma Bâ's forces near Kaolack.  The
battle of Pathebadiane appears to have gone in favor of
the Marabouts, and Pinet-Laprade withdrew his forces

northward. During 1866, Ma Bâ's position in Jolof and the area around Kaolack declined as he was supporting Lat Dior in the invasion of southern Cayor and also his lieutenant, Amer Faal, in action against Niumi. Despite his weakened position, however, Ma Bâ planned to rid himself of the kingdom of Sine, the last Soninke state standing between his kingdom and the French. After the rains began in 1867, Ma Bâ accompanied his army in an invasion of Sine. The Serer tyeddo in a major battle at Somb repulsed the invading forces. Lat Dior fled the area, and after the battle, Ma Bâ's body was discovered on his prayer mat. With Ma Bâ's death, the most critical threat to European power in the Senegambia ended. He had come very close to restoring the old Jolof empire by utilizing the militant forces of Islam which he discovered in Baddibu, Saloum, and Jolof. None of his successors or any other Gambian leader came close to unifying the Senegambia. Ironically, the wars launched by Ma Bâ had weakened the Senegambian states to the extent that the French and British found little resistence to their further penetration of the interior in the following two decades.

BÂ, MAMADOU N'DARE. Chosen by the chiefs of Baddibu to succeed his brother, Ma Bâ, in 1867. Before the wars on the north bank, he had studied the Koran in Mauritania and helped Ma Bâ run a school in Jolof. Like his brother, he was austere and a good puritanical Muslim. He continued the wars begun by Ma Bâ along the Gambia River and reached the apex of his power when he controlled loosely much of the north bank from the Atlantic to Wuli. The British signed a treaty with him, recognizing his hegemony in all those areas except Niumi. However, his Marabout forces were not able to conquer Sine and the inland Wolof territories where the French had become dominant. Mamadou was not successful in establishing permanent institutions of government which could keep his war chiefs in check and in 1877 one of them, Biram Cisse, decided to build his own fortified base and refused Mamadou's order to tear down the walls of his town. This began a devastating civil war which was to last until the French invasion of 1887, when those territories farthest from Nioro were freed from Mamadou's control. Musa Molloh and the Bur Saloum allied themselves with Cisse and by the early 1880s, Mamadou had lost most of the territory over which he had ruled. His problems were

further complicated by the actions of Saër Maty, Ma
Bâ's son, who claimed the kingship created by his
father.   In 1886, the British withdrew the stipend paid
to Mamadou as ruler of Baddibu.   Cisse and Maty had
almost reached an agreement where Cisse recognized
the younger man as suzerain in that year, but each
wanted the stipend which Governor Carter decided to
pay to neither.   The conflict continued into the next
year when French forces defeated the Marabouts,
forced Saër Maty to flee, and divided what was left of
Ma Bâ's patrimony between Cisse and the aged Mamadou.   Once again king, if only over a small area, by
the grace of the French, Mamadou lived to enjoy this
shadow power until his death in 1889.

BÂ, SAËR MATY.   Son of Ma Bâ.   His mother was the
niece of the Burba Jolof.   Although a council of chiefs
had selected his uncle, Mamadou N'Dare Bâ, to succeed
Ma Bâ as ruler of the kingdom of Rip, Saër Maty never
gave wholehearted support to the new ruler.   He had
gained considerable influence by the early 1880s because
of transferred allegiance from his father and also because of his leadership qualities.   It is probable that
he was the real power behind Mamadou before the latter
was so badly defeated by Biram Cisse.   In the mid-
1880s, Saër Maty was involved in a series of wars with
Cisse over control of the riverine areas of Baddibu.
It appeared briefly in 1886 that Cisse would accept the
overlordship of Saër Maty and peace would come to the
north bank.   However, the war continued, and in 1887,
the French, fearful of an extension of the war to
Saloum, decided to pacify the territory.   In April 1887,
the French, reinforced by the tyeddo of Saloum, defeated Saër Maty's forces a number of times, forcing
him to flee to British protection in the Ceded Mile.
The British, concerned with French operations so near
the Gambia River, refused to surrender Saër Maty and
he continued to live quietly in a village near Bathurst
until his death in 1897.

BADDIBU (or, Rip).   Today a section of the Gambia located
on the north bank which stretches roughly from the
town of Salakini to just below the town of Ballangar in
lower Saloum.   The bulk of the present day population
of Baddibu is Mandingo, although there is a significant
concentration of Wolof in upper Baddibu.   In the 19th
century, Baddibu was one of the most important of the

Gambian kingdoms. In the 1860s, Ma Bâ used Baddibu
as his base in attempting to create a large Islamic
kingdom. At its greatest extent, the kingdom of Baddibu, or Rip, comprised not only the present day
riverine areas, but also Saloum, parts of Cayor, and
Jolof.

BADGE MESSENGERS. Created by a Protectorate Ordinance
in 1909 which gave chiefs and certain headmen the
right, with appropriate permission from the British
authorities, to appoint men to keep the peace in a
given area. They were called Badge Messengers because of the peculiar symbol of authority they were
authorized to wear. They had all the rights, duties,
and liabilities of the regular police who operated in
the Colony area. Although conditions in the Protectorate changed drastically in the fifty years after they
were authorized, Badge Messengers remained the local
constabulary which enforced the decisions of the Native
Authorities down to the very eve of independence.

BADOLO. A Wolof term signifying a peasant farmer, the
largest single subdivision of the freeborn caste.

BALDEH, PAUL LOUIS. Teacher and politician, born to a
Fulbe family at Sare N'Gai in 1937 and educated at
local Catholic mission schools and at the Catholic Secondary School at Banjul. In 1954, he attended Dublin
University and received a B. A. degree and returned to
teach at the Banjul Catholic Secondary School. He
early aligned himself with the People's Progressive
Party and resigned his teaching position to campaign
for the party in the upriver Fulbe areas. He was
elected to the House of Assembly in 1962, and received
the portfolio of Minister of Education. Difficulties developed within the party and Baldeh was dismissed in
1963. However, just before independence, he was
again appointed Minister of Education. He was reelected to the House in 1966, but was passed over for
a further ministerial post.

BANJUL. The island ceded by the king of Kombo to Captain
Alexander Grant in 1816 who immediately set his men
building houses and barracks at a site on the island
where a fort could help control entrance into the Gambia estuary. Grant renamed the island St. Mary's and
the new town, Bathurst, in honor of the then Secretary

of State. Banjul Island thus became the center of
British activity in the Gambia and the most populous
portion of the Colony. In 1973, the government of
President Jawara decided to change the name of the
capital city to one without the connotations of the Colonial past. They selected the name Banjul to replace
the old title, Bathurst.

BANTABA. A meeting place, usually a raised platform
under a shade tree in each yard or village where the
elders and the village head would come together to
discuss matters of concern and to arrive at consensus
decisions.

BANTO FARO. A Mandingo term for land areas above river
levels that remain arid in the dry season although they
are flooded during the rains. In the Gambia, these
lands are higher than the mangrove swamps, but lie
below the levels of the sandstone plateau which is an
extension of the soil type found throughout the southern
Senegal and the Casamance. There are two types of
banto faros in the Gambia--the estuarine and the upper
river. The dividing line between the two is found
roughly in the vicinity of Kerewan.

BARRA WAR. In 1827, Burungai Sonko, the king of Barra,
disturbed by Commodore Bullen's decision to build a
fort at Barra Point, decided to abrogate the Ceded
Mile treaty of the previous year. This decision resulted in a number of incidents which culminated in the
important Barra War which did not end until 1831. The
hostilities forced Bullen to stop construction on the fort,
and for a time it appeared that the British would be
driven out of Barra and the Ceded Mile. At one time
the fledgling town of Bathurst was also threatened. The
situation was reversed because the French at Goree
dispatched a warship and troops to aid the British.
This aid allowed the British to recommence construction of Fort Bullen in 1831 which with its three-gun
battery helped to give the British command of the entrance to the Gambia River.

BARRAKUNDA. A town in the Wuli section of the upper
river area of the Gambia. It was the site of the last
of the upper river factories established by English
companies because the falls at Barrakunda marked the
limit of river travel in the dry season. There was a

post established there as early as 1651 which was later destroyed by fire. An English factory was sited there again in 1678 and from time to time traders were posted there as late as 1810.

BATHURST, LORD HENRY. British Secretary of State for Colonies from 1812-1828. Captain Alexander Grant in 1816 named his new town on St. Mary's Island in honor of Bathurst who had authorized the project to restore British prestige on the Gambia River.

BATTIMANSA. Described by Cadamosto in 1456 as the Mandingo ruler of a portion of the north bank approximately sixty miles from the mouth of the Gambia River (probably Baddibu). Battimansa received the Europeans in a very friendly fashion and treated them as honored guests during their 11-day stay, traded with them, and then signed a treaty of friendship.

BINTANG. A village located approximately five miles up the Bintang Bolon from Bintang Point. It was the residence of the king of Foni and was one of the most important trade locales in the 18th century. Both the English and French maintained factories there in the century after 1685. English independent traders continued to use Bintang as a trading base in the early 19th century.

BINTANG BOLON (creek). An important feature noted by early European visitors to the Gambia. It rises south of Elephant Island, north of the watershed of the Casamance River, and flows westward for approximately eighty miles before joining the Gambia River at Bintang Point some thirty miles from St. Mary's Island. It formed the dividing line between Kiang and Foni. From the earliest period of European activity there were always a number of temporary trading stations located along the Bolon. The Royal African Company maintained a major trade factory at Bintang. In some early literature, the stream is referred to as the Geregia River.

BLACKBURNE, SIR KENNETH W. An official of the Colonial Service in the West Indies, seconded to the Gambia to head a five-man development committee appointed by Governor Southorn in 1940. This committee was the Gambia's response to a Colonial Office directive that all

colonies and territories prepare detailed analyses of
the needs of the separate segments of the Empire and
make recommendations for use of Colonial Development
and Welfare Funds at the conclusion of World War II.
The Blackburn Report issued in 1943 was the first
logical statement of the Gambia's needs which encom-
passed all areas of the economy.  The report, although
many of its recommendations were ignored, served as
the guide for Gambian development between 1945-1950.

BLOOD, SIR HILARY.  Governor of the Gambia during the
latter stages of World War II and immediately afterward, from 1942-1947.  His administration was responsible for drawing up proposals for the improvements of the Colony area utilizing Colonial Development and Welfare Funds.  Although these funds fell
short of expectations, the modernization of the water
supply, the sewage system, paved streets and improvements of the port date to Blood's administration.  Later
Sir Hilary became governor of Malta and was the director of the United Nations-sponsored plebicite in the
British Cameroon.

BOJANG, TOMANI.  The last Soninke king of the Kombo.
After being hard pressed by the Marabout dissidents
at Gunjur in 1863-64, he agreed to the truce with Fodi
Kabba and Fodi Silla arranged by Governor D'Arcy.
For over half a decade there was relative peace between the two factions in Kombo, broken only by sporadic violence.  In 1870, Tomani Bojang, upon learning
of the proposed cession of British territories to the
French, addressed a dignified note to the Queen re-
questing that if she no longer wanted those areas deeded
to her that she could "return my territory back to me
as an act of friendship."  The British government informed him that it could not accede to his request.  In
the troubled years of the 1870s neither could the British
protect him completely from his Marabout enemies who
had become even more powerful.  Hostilities broke out
in 1871, and within two years all of the Soninke towns
in Kombo with the exception of Busumballa and Brikama
were in Soninke hands.  In the following year, Bojang
lost Brikama, and a small remnant of his territory was
saved only by a British arranged truce in 1874.  In the
following year, Fodi Silla began the war again and his
forces took Basumballa, forcing the king to take refuge
at Lamin, within a few yards of British territory.  The

British Administrator, fearing that war would spread
to British Kombo, warned Tomani Bojang not to expect
any British aid. The king, therefore, was forced to
accept Fodi Silla's humiliating terms. He shaved his
head, became a Muslim, and tore down his stockade.
His old enemy then allowed him enough land for himself and his people, in the territory which Bojang's
dynasty had ruled for over two centuries.

BOOKER, JOHN.  Chief agent of the Royal African Company
in the Gambia from 1688 until his death in mid-1693.
He was one of the most loyal and successful of the
company servants in Africa.  The outbreak of the war
with France in 1689 found him in charge of fewer than
200 men and no ships of war permanently stationed on
the river.  Nevertheless, he used visiting company vessels to drive French shipping from the coast, to deal
with privateers, and finally to transport an expeditionary
force against St. Louis and Goree.  Both French stations were captured in December 1692, their stores
seized, and their defenses demolished.  His death by
fever removed the one company man who might have
resisted the French forces which recaptured St. Louis
and Goree in 1693.

BRAVO, MAJOR ALEXANDER.  Acting Administrator of the
Gambia in 1870 who attempted to rebutt the arguments
of local and British merchants against the exchange of
the Gambia for suitable French territory elsewhere.

BRIDGES, PHILIP R.  Civil servant and solicitor, born in
England in 1922.  He was educated at Aberdeen Uni-
versity and served with the Royal Artillery attached to
the West African Frontier Force in Burma during World
War II.  He was posted to the Gambia in 1954 as so-
licitor to the Supreme Court and later served in the
Attorney-General's office.  In 1964 he was appointed
Attorney-General, a post he continued to hold after inde-
pendence, being the only European in the Gambia's
Ministry.

BRITISH WEST AFRICAN SETTLEMENTS.  Until 1843, the
administration of Sierra Leone and the Gambia was the
primary responsibility of a governor resident at Freetown.  The Gambia was administered directly by an
Administrator subordinate to his chief in Sierra Leone.
In 1843 the administration of each territory became the

province of a governor resident in each locale, and
thus the Gambia was severed from direct connection
with Sierra Leone.   One of the major results of the
Parliamentary investigations of 1865 was to return to
the older system, placing all the British territories—
Sierra Leone, Gambia, the Gold Coast, and Lagos--
under one governor with overall responsibility.   Thus
the administration of the Gambia became subordinate
to decisions made in Freetown.   In 1874 the British
possessions on the Gold Coast and at Lagos were
separated from Sierra Leone, but the Gambia remained
under the control of the governor of the British West
African Settlements.   It was not until November 1888
that the Gambia was released from this cumbersome
and economically debilitating dependence, and it became
a separate Colony.

BROWN, THOMAS.   British merchant whose firm was one of
the largest in the Gambia in the late 1860s and early
1870s.   Brown and Company had been trading in the
hinterland since the early 1830s and Brown had made
enough money to retire to England in 1854.   However,
five years later he was back and soon his agents were
challenging French firms for supremacy on the lower
Gambia River.   He was a member of the Legislative
Council during much of that period of early negotiations
with France over exchanging the Gambia.   He was one
of the chief opponents to both attempts by Britain to be
rid of the Gambia.   He wrote long polemical letters,
signed memorials, and personally lobbied at the Colonial
Office against the trade since he was convinced that
British and African firms would not receive adequate
compensation and would be forced out of business by the
French.   Brown and Company continued in operation until 1880 and Brown was the last of the pioneer British
merchants to continue to reside in Bathurst.

BRUE, ANDRE.   Director-General of the French Senegal
Company after 1697, with his headquarters at St. Louis.
He was dedicated to driving English traders from the
Senegambia and gaining French dominance of trade on
the Gambia River.   However, he was not able to accom-
plish this despite a quarter of a century of effort directed toward this end.   Major reasons for his failure
were his inability to control piracy, the losses sustained
by the Senegal Company during the War of Spanish Succession, and the growing economic weaknesses of the
Company.

BULLEN, CHARLES. A Commodore in the British Navy and a veteran of Trafalgar who in 1826 was in command of HMS Maidstone which arrived in the Gambia to support the acting Governor of Sierra Leone, Kenneth MacAulay, in his negotiations with Burungai Sonko, the king of Barra. Subsequently a treaty was signed ceding to Britain the whole right bank of the river one mile inland from Jinnak Creek to Jokadu Creek. Immediately after the signing, Commodore Bullen transported two cannon to Barra Point. A military guard was placed over these guns and the site was named Fort Bullen in honor of the Commodore.

BUR. The title of the king in the Serer states of Sine and Saloum.

BURBA. The title given to the king in the earliest dominant Wolof state of Jolof.

BURTON, SIR RICHARD. A distinguished 19th-century explorer, translator, and author. As British Consul to Fernando Po, he visited the Gambia in 1863 and left his impressions of Bathurst and the British government in a book, Wanderings in West Africa from Liverpool to Fernando Po under the pseudonymous initials F. R. G. S.

BUSUMBULLA. A town in Kombo midway between Sukuta and Brikama which was the main fortified base of the rulers. By mid-1874, Busumbulla was the only town loyal to the Soninke king, Tomani Bojang. Its capture in the following year forced him to capitulate and accept Islam in exchange for the right to continue to live in Kombo.

-C-

CD&W    see    COLONIAL DEVELOPMENT AND WELFARE ACTS

CDC    see    COLONIAL DEVELOPMENT CORPORATION

CADAMOSTO, ALVISE DA. A Venetian captain employed by Prince Henry of Portugal, commissioned in 1455 to investigate rumors of lands along the Gambia River where great quantities of gold could be obtained. Sailing in a

90-ton ship, he was joined off Cape Verde by Antoniotto
Usidimare with two ships, and together they entered the
estuary of the Gambia River.  Armed resistance from
Africans in canoes so unnerved the crews that they refused to proceed further.  In the following year, Cadamosto returned with three ships to the Gambia and
proceeded approximately sixty miles upriver.  He was
warmly received by the Mandingo ruler of Baddibu,
concluded a treaty of friendship with him, and acquired
a few slaves and some gold in their trading.  After
staying in Baddibu for 11 days, he sailed down river,
explored the southern coastline as far as the Casamance River, and then returned to Portugal.

CAMARA, ANDREW DAVID.  A politician, born at Mansa-
    jang in the upper river region in 1923.  He is a Fulbe
    convert to Christianity and was educated in the Pro-
    tectorate and Bathurst.  He was a teacher for 10 years
    before entering politics in 1958.  Camara was elected
    in 1960 as an Independent member of the House of
    Assembly.  He shifted to the United Party and served
    as minister when P. S. N'Jie was Chief Minister.  In
    1962, he again changed his party affiliation to the PPP
    and was returned to the House with a large majority.
    He was named Minister of Education in 1963 and held
    that position for many years.  He was appointed Minis-
    ter of External Affairs to succeed A. B. N'Jie, a post
    which he continued to hold in 1973.

CAMERON, SIR EDWARD J.  Governor of the Gambia during
    World War I, serving from 1914 to 1920.  He was
    responsible for putting into effect the provisions of the
    Comprehensive Protectorate Ordinance of 1913.  In
    1919, he issued another Protectorate Ordinance which
    further defined relative powers of the central govern-
    ment and the chiefs, and also introduced a new scale
    of Protectorate taxes.  It was during Cameron's tenure
    of office that British firms gained supremacy in trade
    from their French competitors.  The failure of Cameron
    and his successor, C. H. Armitage, to act quickly to
    equalize the exchange rate for the five franc piece
    eventually cost the Gambia over £200,000.

CARTER, SIR GILBERT.  Administrator of the Gambia from
    1888 to 1891.  During his short term of office, Britain
    reversed its decades old policy against territorial ex-
    pansion.  In 1888, Carter was ordered to enter into

definite treaties of cession with Gambian chiefs.  His
recommendation to his superiors that they claim a
large segment of the hinterland of the Gambia River
was largely ignored by the delegates to the Paris Conference in 1889.  After the declaration of the Protectorate,  Carter with his small force and few resources
could do little but announce the change to the upper
and middle river Gambian chiefs.

CASAMANCE.  A small area lying between the Gambia and
Guinea Bissau.  It is one of the seven administrative
regions of the Republic of Senegal, almost completely
separated from the rest of the state by the Gambia.
The upper and middle portions of the territory belong
to the Sahel zone while the lower Casamance marks the
beginning of the West African rain forest zone.  Inhabited by Papel, Balante, Tucolor, Fulbe, and Mandingo,
the present day Casamance was historically a part of
the Gambia River complex and it was not until 1889
that it was arbitrarily separated from the Gambia.

CEDED MILE.  In June 1826, Kenneth MacAulay, acting
Governor of Sierra Leone, negotiated with Burungai
Sonko, the king of Barra, the cession to the Crown of
a coastal strip, one mile in depth beginning at Jinnak
Creek on the west as far as Jokadu Creek to the east.
In January 1832, following the Barra War, this cession
was reconfirmed and the area controlled by the British
was extended slightly.  The Ceded Mile was administered by the British as a part of the Colony, even after
the declaration of a Protectorate over the hinterland
areas in 1889.

CHOWN, THOMAS, SR.  British merchant who formed a
family-owned trading company which operated in the
Gambia from the early 1830s.  He combined his efforts with those of other British merchants such as
T. F. Quin and Thomas Brown, and Gambian traders
like J. D. Cole and E. J. Nicol to oppose the 1866-
1870 plan to cede the Gambia to France.

CHOWN, THOMAS, JR.  British merchant who had taken
control of the family business interests in the Gambia
in 1870.  He was one of the 10 members of the Gambia
Committee which lobbied successfully in 1875 and 1876
against the revived plan of the Colonial Office to exchange the Gambia for French territory.

CHURCH OF ENGLAND. Its activities in the Gambia date
from 1821 when at the request of Sir Charles Mac-
Carthy, a chaplain was sent for the Bathurst garrison.
However, due to the high mortality rate, there was
normally no Anglican representative in Bathurst during
the first half of the 19th century. In 1836, the government allowed Anglicans to use the former officers'
mess for church services. No permanent church in
Bathurst was erected until the present structure was
built in 1901. In 1855, missionary work was begun by
the Anglican Church of the West Indies among the
Susus along the Rio Pongas. In 1935, this area was
combined with that of the Gambia and the first Bishop
for this new diocese was appointed. Although not as
active in the education field as the Wesleyans, the
Anglicans did open a church school in Bathurst as
early as 1869 and maintained from the 1920s one small
elementary school in the Protectorate.

CISSE, BIRAM. Born into an important Marabout family at
Kaur, he early came under the influence of Ma Bâ and
proved himself one of the better military leaders of the
kingdom of Rip. After Ma Bâ's death, he precipitated
a rebellion against Momadou N'Dare Bâ by refusing to
dismantle his fortifications at Kaur. He was aided in
his struggle against Momadou by Musa Molloh and by
the Bur Saloum, Guedel M'Bodj. By the early 1880s,
Cisse had managed to drive Momadou from most of
the vast territory he had once controlled. Complica-
tions arose, however, when Saër Maty, the son of Ma
Bâ, claimed the throne of Baddibu and Cisse found
this new enemy more formidable than Momadou. Despite considerable military success, particularly in the
campaign of 1885, he was unable to completely defeat
Saër Maty, and in 1886, agreed to the proposal of
British mediators to accept Saër Maty as his suzerain
provided he could keep his territory and receive a
stipend from the British. When the latter was not
forthcoming, Cisse refused the agreement. In the civil
war, both parties had encroached on the territory of
Saloum and the French, fearing a recurrence of Rip
domination there, sent a military column against Saër
Maty in 1887, defeated his armies, and forced him to
flee. Cisse was not involved directly in this action and
received from the French guarantees of a part of the
kingdom of Rip. However, after rumors of an impend-
ing renewal of violence reached him, the French

Commandant at Nioro arrested Cisse in June 1888 and
he was exiled to Gabon.

CLOSER ASSOCIATION. Relates to the offical attempts and
private views concerned with political, social, and economic reunification of the Senegambia. Serious consideration was given to this question by the British even
before the constitutional advances of the 1960s. The
British and Senegalese did not want to appear to force
Gambia into an unwanted association, but rejoining the
two areas seemed an obvious solution to the economic
non-viability of the Gambia, and it would rectify the
arbitrary division established by the Anglo-French Convention of 1889. In 1961, an interministerial committee was created by President Senghor and P. S. N'Jie
to examine ways toward a practical union of the two
polities. A United Nations report favored some form
of ultimate political union in order to raise the economic level of both countries. The public statements
of the leaders of France, Britain, and Senegal indicated
their approval of closer association. A treaty of association between Senegal and Gambia was also signed in
the early 1960s. Despite the continued meetings of the
interministerial committee and promises of economic
cooperation, little has been done to achieve union. The
PPP leadership fears that Gambia will be dominated in
any federation by the Senegalese; Gambia's economic
position has improved while Senegal's has worsened;
Senegal's politics are complex and far from stable;
Gambia has shown, since 1965, that it can exist by itself. Thus in many ways, practical political association is presently as far away as it was a decade ago.

COLONIAL DEVELOPMENT AND WELFARE ACTS (CD&W).
The first of these acts was passed by the British Parliament in early 1940 and represented a reversal of the
previous doctrine for the Dependent Empire. Instead of
demanding fiscal self-sufficiency of all territories, Parliament recognized a responsibility to aid in developing
all of its territories even though an area might not itself have the available funds. Under these acts, Britain, although hard-pressed in the years immediately
after World War II, made massive grants of funds to
its African territories. Although falling far short of
expectations, the Gambia in the decade after 1957 received over £$1\frac{1}{2}$ million from Colonial Development and
Welfare funds. These funded the construction of a new

bridge, a high school, Victoria Hospital, and a better
water supply, paved streets, and an adequate drainage
system for the capital city. The bulk of the funds al-
located for the Protectorate went for the improvement
of agriculture and building an asphalt road from Brikama to Mansa Konko and construction of the hospital at
Bansang.

COLONIAL DEVELOPMENT CORPORATION (CDC). Created
by the British government in 1948 to devise development schemes which would secure the dual purpose of
providing necessary income for the territories and also
a profit for the corporation. The direction of the corporation was the responsibility of a Board of Directors
of eight members with Lord Trefgarne as chairman.
The corporation was concerned with funding two major
projects in the Gambia. The first was a large-scale
mechanized project to clear land, plant, and harvest
rice mechanically on 4700 acres of land near Wallikunda. The project was not successful and after the
expenditure of great sums, the facilities were taken
over in 1953 by the Gambian government which continued to operate the farm as an experimental station.
The other project of the corporation in the Gambia was
even more expensive and glaringly unsuccessful. From
1948 to early 1951, the corporation expended nearly one
million pounds in the Yundum egg scheme. A combination of factors--poor management, over optimistic estimates of profits, failure to confer with local officials,
and chicken disease--combined to make the Yundum
project one of the corporation's greatest African failures.

COMPANY OF MERCHANTS TRADING TO AFRICA (British).
Created by an act of Parliament in 1750, it was the
successor to the bankrupt Royal African Company which,
however, was not divested of all its powers until 1752.
The Company of Merchants was prohibited from all
trading in its corporate capacity. It was directed by
an appointed executive committee empowered to make
rules regarding trading in West Africa and which thus
could charge trading fees and customs duties. It received an annual subsidy from Parliament for the maintenance of the trading forts and stations. The Crown
exercised supervisory control over the activities of the
company. The fort on James Island was repaired and
restaffed, and with the aid of ships of the British navy,
French attempts to dominate Gambian trade from Albreda

were thwarted even before the outbreak of the Seven
Years War. During that war, the British beat off a
French attack on James Island in 1757, and in the following year captured and garrisoned all the main
French bases in Senegal. At the outbreak of the war,
the company had relinquished its rights of administration. Its territories were administered by the military
until 1765 when the Colony of the Senegambia was created with its centrum at St. Louis. During the War
for American Independence, a French force reoccupied
St. Louis and razed James Fort in early 1779. The
Treaty of Versailles of 1783 restored to the French all
they had lost in the Senegambia, and in the same year
the Crown turned over to the Company of Merchants
control over the Gambia area. The company showed
no great zeal in reestablishing trade relations. Parliament many times refused a grant which the company
directors felt necessary for the reconstruction of James
Fort, and it was never rebuilt. British trade on the
river was maintained by private merchants. Finally in
1816, the Crown decided to send Captain Alexander
Grant with a small party to build a fort near the river's
mouth whose main function would be to control the
slave trade. The Company of Merchants did not under-
write this venture, and there developed in theory, a
duality of control. Finally in 1821, all the forts and
territories were taken from the company and placed
under the direct jurisdiction of the Crown.

CONFERENCE OF PROTECTORATE CHIEFS. An annual
meeting of the seyfolu of the Gambia was instituted in
1944 as a means of better communication with the governor and the central agencies of the administration.
The conferences which were held at different locales
each year were occasions of great pomp and ceremony.
The meetings all followed a similar format. The governor would address the chiefs, outlining his proposals for
action for the coming year. This would be followed by
presentations by the heads of the central departments of
their activities during the previous year and their plans
for the coming year. Until 1958, the chiefs did not
take an active role, asked few questions, and accepted
the government's predetermined policy without demur.
From 1958 onward, a number of chiefs, at times vehemently, began to comment and question the performance
of the government. However, political parties soon
supplanted the chiefs as the dominant spokesmen for the

Protectorate and the conference never became more
than a passive sounding board for the central administration.

CONTON, WILLIAM. Novelist and educator, born in 1925 in
Bathurst where his father was a clergyman. He was
educated in the Gambia and Sierra Leone before leaving
for university training at Durham in England. After
receiving his B.A., he returned to West Africa where
he became the principal of the Government Secondary
School at Bo in Sierra Leone. He is the author of The
African published in 1960, one of the first novels by
an African to gain worldwide circulation and acclaim.

COURLAND, DUCHY OF. An independent Baltic Duchy in
the 17th century under the suzerainty of the kings of
Poland. James, Duke of Courland, caught up in mer-
cantilistic dreams of the wealth of Guinea, formed a
trading company in 1650. In the following year his
agents leased Banjul from the king of Kombo, a small
plot of land at Juffure on the north bank, and most important, an island in the Gambia River from the king
of Barra. The island was named St. Andrews (later
renamed James Island by the British). The company
sent a group of settlers under Major Fock who built an
excellent fort on the island from whence the Courlanders
hoped to dominate the river trade. The Duke's dream
of a mercantile empire based on the Gambia and the
West Indies were dashed by the corruption of his lieutenants and the open hostility of greater European
powers and the events in the Baltic. The Duke was
captured by Charles X of Sweden in 1658 and he assigned the rights to manage his Gambian holdings to
the Dutch West Indies Company. In 1661, St. Andrews
Island was captured by the English under Major Robert
Holmes. In 1664, Courland ceded its rights in the
Gambia to England in return for a guarantee to respect
the Duke's control over Tobago in the West Indies.

-D-

DCA    see  DEMOCRATIC CONGRESS ALLIANCE

DP    see  DEMOCRATIC PARTY

DABO, DARI BANA. The Marabout chief of Sankandi and a

follower of Fodi Kabba in the late 1890s.   When the
long-standing quarrel over rice lands with the Soninkes
of Jataba became critical, Travelling Commissioner
F. C. Sitwell investigated and awarded the lands to
Jataba.   Dari Bana Dabo refused to be bound by this
decision and decided to fight when Sitwell, accompanied
by Commissioner Silva and 11 African constables, appeared at Sankandi in early 1900 to enforce the award.
In the ensuing skirmish, the two Travelling Commissioners, a neighboring chief, and six constables were
killed.   As soon as troops were available, the British
in conjunction with the French moved to pacify those
areas loyal to Fodi Kabba.   French troops moved on
Medina, Fodi Kabba's stronghold, in March 1901.   The
British allied with Musa Molloh had already taken Sankandi in January.   Dari Bana Dabo fled to French territory where he was captured and turned over to the
British for trial.   He and two of his lieutenants were
tried before the Supreme Court in Bathurst and found
guilty of the deaths of Sitwell and his party.   Dari
Bana Dabo was sentenced to death and executed.

D'ARCY, G. A. K. (Colonel).   Succeeded Lieutenant-Colonel
    O'Connor as Governor of the Gambia in 1859.   He ar-
    rived in the midst of a yellow fever epidemic which
    had reduced the European population of Bathurst to
    fewer than a dozen persons.   His pleas to the Colonial
    Office for extra funds to be able to drain Half Die and
    improve the sanitation facilities of the Colony fell on
    deaf ears and many of his recommendations were not
    carried into effect a half-century later.   D'Arcy's
    expedition against Baddibu in 1861 set in motion the
    series of events which brought Ma Bâ to power.   Through-
    out his tenure, D'Arcy was constrained from any policy
    toward Ma Bâ and the middle and upper river areas
    which would have committed the British government to
    any more expense.   The treaty of friendship D'Arcy
    signed with Ma Bâ in February 1863 concerning Niumi
    was a good example of the type of intervention D'Arcy
    was limited to.   Although some of Ma Bâ's lieutenants
    continued to cause trouble in Niumi, Ma Bâ kept his
    word and did not again disturb the area.   In the Kom-
    bos, D'Arcy had the force to confront the Marabouts
    and Fodi Kabba, and to maintain an uneasy status quo
    through 1864 and 1865.   The chief disturber of the peace
    was Amer Faal who raided into the Ceded Mile.   In July
    1866, with naval support and 500 reinforcements from

Essau, D'Arcy's West Indian troops stormed Tubab
Kolon, Amer Faal's strongpoint.  D'Arcy's ideas concerning British influence in the Senegambia were reflected in the report of Colonel St. George Ord in
1865, but aside from a few punitive forays such as
Tubab Kolon, D'Arcy could do little to increase British
control along the river.

DE JASPAS, MELCHOIR.  An Armenian resident of Great
   Britain who was used by the Royal African Company to
   translate some of Job ben Solomon's Arabic letters.
   The company decided to use his language skills and
   sent him to the Gambia in 1737.   Because of maltreat-
   ment, he left the company in the following year.   However, in 1740 he was reemployed and accompanied Job
   ben Solomon to Bondu.   In 1744 he journeyed overland
   to Cachau in Portuguese Guinea.   Little of concrete
   trading value was obtained for the company by de
   Jaspas in his explorations, perhaps because the outbreak of war with France in 1743 focused the company's
   attention elsewhere.

DEMA.   Wolof term for witches, whom they fear greatly.
   A person becomes a dema through his mother.   If the
   mother is a witch, then the children are also suspected
   of being able to do great harm.   Witches are believed
   to be able to take animal or bird form and to eat people's souls and drink their blood.

DEMOCRATIC CONGRESS ALLIANCE (DCA).   Formed in
   1960 by a merger of the Democratic Party and the
   Muslim Congress because the leaders of the older
   parties, Reverend J. C. Faye and I. M. Garba-Jahumpa, wanted a stronger, Protectorate-wide party to contest the elections against the United Party and the People's Progressive Party.   However, only three of their
   candidates were elected to the House of Representatives
   in 1960.   In 1961 the DCA leaders reached an agreement with Jawara and the PPP, and although there was
   no merger, the DCA cooperated with the PPP for the
   elections of 1962.   Despite the victory of the PPP, the
   DCA could win only one seat in the expanded House of
   Representatives.   This failure and differences of political philosophy between Garba-Jahumpa and Faye soon
   led to the breakup of the DCA.

DEMOCRATIC PARTY (DP) .   The first political party in the

Gambia. It was formed in February 1951, by the adherents of Reverend John C. Faye to contest for one
of the Bathurst seats in the Legislative Council under
the provisions of the Constitution of that year. It was
successful in returning Reverend Faye to office. In
the 1950s, this Colony based party was the vehicle by
which Reverend Faye successfully opposed his political
rivals, I. M. Garba-Jahumpa and P. S. N'Jie.
However, Faye came to be considered by his constitu-
ents as a tool of the British colonial regime. This
factor and the extension of the elections to the Protectorate in 1960 deeply undercut the influence of the
Democratic Party. Prior to the elections of 1960, it
was merged with the Muslim Congress to form the
Democratic Congress Alliance. The failure of this
coalition in the two elections of 1960 and 1962 resulted
in strains between the leaders, and I. M. Garba-
Jahumpa withdrew and reconstituted the Muslim Congress. Many of Reverend Faye's adherents shifted
their allegiance to either the People's Progressive
Party or the United Party, and the Democratic Party
was not revived.

DEMONETIZATION. The crisis over the exchange of the
five franc piece in the Gambia after World War I
caused the British government in January 1922 to re-
deem all those coins then in circulation at the legal
rate. The legal rate in the Gambia was approximately
1 3/4 times the world rate. Failure of the government to act soon caused the demonetization to cost
over £2,000,000 more than if these coins had been
redeemed at the world rate. The cost of demonetization was borne by the poor government of the
Gambia.

DENTON, SIR GEORGE C. The first chief executive of the
modern era in the Gambia to be commissioned by the
Colonial Office as Governor instead of Administrator.
He completed the work begun by his successor, Sir R.
B. Llewellyn, in devising the framework of British
rule in the Protectorate. This was done by a series
of Protectorate Ordinances which refined and clarified
the earlier system. The most important of these
Ordinances was that of 1902 and two modifying ones in
1909. Denton's main contribution to the Gambia was
his resistence to the requirements of the Anglo-British
Convention of 1904 which would have assigned a mid-river

port on the Gambia River to the French. His arguments that such a cession would destroy the British
and Gambian merchants at Bathurst had considerable
influence in determining the dilatory attitude of the
Home government in delaying the cession until after
World War I when subsequent events made the French
abandon their designs on the middle river areas. He
served as Governor of the Gambia from 1900 to 1911.

DIBBA, SHERIF MUSTAPHA. A politician, born in 1937,
the son of a farmer at Salikini. His father in the
early 1960s became chief of Central Baddibu. Dibba
was educated in government and mission schools and
worked briefly as a clerk for the United Africa Company until he resigned in 1959 to work for the advancement of the People's Progressive Party. He was particularly active in organizing the youth wing of the
party. He was elected to the House of Assembly in
1960 and returned in all subsequent elections. In 1964
he became Minister of Labor and in the following year
Minister of Local Government. After the 1966 elections, he was appointed Minister of Works and Communications. After Sherif Sisay was expelled from the
PPP, Dibba was selected to be the Minister of Finance.
When Gambia became a Republic in 1970, he was
chosen to be Vice-President while continuing as Finance
Minister. He relinquished the latter portfolio in early
1973.

DIEPPE MERCHANTS. They were the first French traders
to trade openly with Cape Verde, the Gambia, and the
Guinea coast despite Portuguese claims to a monopoly
of trade in all of western Africa. By 1560, they had
established regular trade with Cape Verde and in 1570,
the first French ship entered the Gambia River.

DIOUF, COUMBA N'DOFFÈNE. Bur Sine from 1853 to 1871
whose position in the 1860s was threatened from two
external forces. The French, following a gradual process of extending their authority into the hinterland,
had come to dominate the Wolof states of Baol, Walo,
and Cayor to the north. Ma Bâ's armies had conquered
much of the north bank kingdoms of the Gambia, Saloum,
and Jolof. Sine was thus directly threatened by the
raids of Ma Bâ's lieutenants, although for six years
Ma Bâ avoided a direct confrontation with the tyeddo of
Sine. Coumba N'Doffène resisted French attempts to

act as the French cat's paw against Ma Bâ.   However,
in 1867, Ma Bâ decided to rid himself of the threat of
the "pagans" and led a large army into Sine.   In one
of the most decisive battles in the western Sudan in the
19th century, Coumba N'Doffène's troops defeated the
Marabouts, Ma Bâ was killed, and within a short time
the threat from a unified interior Islamic kingdom had
disappeared.   Coumba N'Doffène's later attempts to
extend Sine's control over neighboring areas ended
tragically with his death by gunshot at Joal in 1871.

DOG  ISLAND.   A small island located near the right bank
of the Gambia River approximately mid-way between
Barra Point and Lamin Point.   In the 18th century it
was called Charles Island by the British.   Much of the
stone used in the permanent buildings in early day
Bathurst was quarried here since the king of Niumi
gave Captain Alexander Grant permission to transport
stone from Dog Island.

DUTCH  WEST  INDIES  COMPANY   see   WEST  INDIES
COMPANY  (DUTCH)

-E-

ELEPHANT  ISLAND.   A large island located approximately
100 miles from the ocean at approximately 15° 20'
longitude where the Gambia River begins a great bend
to the north.   It briefly divides the river into two
channels.   Above Elephant Island the water is normally
not saline.

EROPINA.   One of the nine Mandingo kingdoms located
along the south bank of the Gambia River.   Eropina
was one of the smaller polities located opposite Deer
Island.   During the Soninke-Marabout Wars, it was
conquered by Alfa Molloh and incorporated into his
kingdom of Fuladu.   In the 20th century reorganization
of the Protectorate, the area which was Eropina was
joined to the old kingdom of Niamina and this composite was divided into three segments each under the
direction of a chief.

EXECUTIVE  COUNCIL.   One of the two councils utilized in
British colonies to assist the governor in making decisions.   From 1843 to 1866, the Gambia had a small

nominated Executive Council. There was no council
during the period from 1866 until the nominated council was reconstituted in 1888. The official or government appointees constituted a majority. No provision
was made for members of the Executive Council to be
responsible to a legislative unit, and it remained advisory until being phased out by the new constitutional
instruments just prior to independence.

-F-

FACTOR. An agent of a Chartered Company who was given
the responsibility for disposing of trade goods for the
company. The chief factors for most of the British
companies in the Gambia also were held responsible
for administering James Fort and the outlying trading
stations, and applying the common law to all Europeans
in their jurisdiction. Although the position was primarily commercial, many factors, particularly during
the century-long rivalry between France and Britain,
were forced to assume military command as well.

FAIDHERBE, GENERAL LOUIS L. C. Governor of Senegal
from 1854-1861 and from 1863-1865. He was one of
the designers of the early French forward policy in
West Africa. In his first term, he improved the economic structure of the small colony, constructed an
efficient small African army, defeated the southern
Mauritanian sheikhs, and sponsored the activities of
French merchants in the peanut producing areas of
Cayor, Sine, and Saloum. It was Faidherbe's new
found strength which checked the westward movement
of Al Hajj Umar in the middle Senegal River region.
By pressing for the building of a telegraph line to link
St. Louis to Dakar, he committed France to a policy
of interference in Cayor and Baol, and by constructing
forts in the Serer states, extended French influence almost to the banks of the Gambia River. Faidherbe and
his successors in the 1860s followed a shifting policy
of diplomacy and power in helping to check the expansionist activities of Ma Bâ. The defeat of Ma Bâ at
Somb by the Sine tyeddo represented a vindication of
French policy and laid the groundwork for eventual
French expansion into the deep hinterland of the Senegambia.

FANAL. The Portuguese word meaning a lighthouse or lantern, but which today refers to the building of lightweight wood and paper model ships by differing Muslim and Christian societies. These highly detailed ships are lighted by candles and are the focal point for a major celebration and parade through all the major streets of Banjul on Christmas Eve.

FARBANNA. The eldest son of the appropriate lineage in the 19th-century state of Wuli. He had greater political influence than king's sons in other Mandingo states and lived in a separate fortified compound in the chief town.

FAYE, JOHN COLLEY. Educator, minister, and politician, born in Bathurst in 1908. He was educated at St. Mary's Anglican School and the Methodist Boys High School. He received a first class teacher's certificate in 1927 and became a tutor at the Methodist Boys High School. From 1932-34 he was headmaster of Methodist Central School before transferring to St. Mary's Anglican School where he became headmaster in 1938. Four years later he became the headmaster of Krista Kunda School in the Protectorate and held this position until 1948. In 1947, he became a deacon of the Anglican Commission and received an M.B.E. for his pioneering work in education. He was elected to the Bathurst Town Council first in 1940, and returned three times unopposed before his posting upriver. From November 1947 to February 1951, he represented the upper river area as a nominated member of the Legislative Council. In February 1951, he was instrumental in creating the Democratic Party, the first political party in the Gambia, and was elected to the Legislative Council at the head of the poll. In the subsequent elections in the 1950s, Faye was reelected to the Council and served until June 1960. From 1954 until 1960, he served as ministerial head of Works and Communications. In 1960, Faye joined the Democratic Party with the Muslim Congress Party of I. M. Garba-Jahumpa to form the Democratic Congress Alliance. Despite this merger, Faye was defeated for election to the House of Assembly. He was leader of the DCA until 1963 when Garba-Jahumpa broke up the coalition. In 1963-64, Faye was the Gambian Commissioner to the United Kingdom.

FINDEN, HARRY.  A very successful trader and merchant
in Bathurst during the third quarter of the 19th century.  Barely literate, he was, nevertheless, elected
leader of the Igbo Friendly Society in 1849 in succession to Thomas Reffell.  He was one of the most important Gambians in the protest movement of the 1870s
against Britain's proposed exchange of the Gambia for
French territory.  In concert with Joseph Reffell,
Thomas Brown, and J. D. Richards, he helped design
and sign the many memorials to the British government officials in Bathurst and London stating the opposition of the Bathurst trading community to any such
exchange.

FITZGERALD, CHARLES.  Secretary of the Gambia Committee which opposed the cession of the Gambia to France
in 1875-76.  He was a retired officer of the West
Indies Regiment who in 1875 authored a widely circu-
lated pamphlet entitled The Gambia and Its Proposed
Cession to France.  It is probable that he had written
an earlier pamphlet issued anonymously in 1870 entitled Has the Crown the Right to Cede the Gambia to
France?

FIVE FRANC PIECE.  A very handsome French coin which
was accepted by an Order-in-Council as legal tender
in the Gambia.  The exchange rate was set at three
shillings, ten and one-half pence.  By the opening of
the 20th century, it comprised over 80 per cent of the
total money in circulation in the Gambia.  By the end
of World War I, the franc had fallen in value, but
nothing was done in the Gambia to make the official
rate conform to the world rate.  Issuance of the new
West African alloyed coins in 1920 did not drive out
the older currency.  The Gambia was the only place
in the world where the five franc piece could be ex-
changed at a rate approximately 1 3/4 times its real
value, and the area was thus flooded by the coins.
They ceased to be valid for overseas transfers in
March 1921, and in April their importation was prohibited.  These actions did not halt the influx of the
coins.  Eventually in 1922, the British decided to de-
monetize, and called in all the five franc pieces at the
legal rate.  The cost of the failure of British authorities to act promptly had to be borne by the Gambia.
The demonetization cost the Gambia over £200,000 at

a time when social and economic improvements were
being denied ostensibly because of a lack of funds.

FONI.   One of the nine Mandingo kingdoms along the south
bank of the Gambia River in the early 19th century,
lying south of Bintang Bolon and adjoining Kombo in
the west.   During the latter stages of the Soninke-
Marabout Wars, the traditional rulers were overthrown
and most of the territory was controlled by adherents
of either Fodi Kabba or Fodi Silla.  However, the
large Jola population resident there resisted conversion
and was never completely conquered.   In 1887, most
of the Jola chiefs placed themselves under British protection and seven years later after Fodi Silla's defeat,
they refused sanctuary to his forces, forcing him to
flee to the Casamance.   The non-Jola leaders also assumed a pro-British position in the 1890s, thus de-
priving Fodi Kabba of much needed support.   In the
20th-century British reorganization of the Protectorate,
Foni was divided into six districts--Foni Brefet, Foni
Bintang, Foni Karani, Foni Kansala, Foni Bondali, and
Foni Jarrol--each under the direction of a chief.

FOON, KEBBA WALLY.   A Bathurst accountant and Wolof
political leader, born in 1922 and educated at the Boys
High School in Bathurst.   He worked as a junior clerk
in the Treasury Department and on the Gambian
steamers of the travelling Post Office.   Early in World
War II he joined the merchant marine and in 1945 received an appointment to Posts and Telecommunications
in London.   From 1948 to 1952 he served as clerk-
accountant in the British Ministry of Agriculture.   Becoming a certified accountant, he joined a firm of London chartered accountants, and in 1954 returned to the
Gambia to establish their office in Bathurst.   In 1955
he started his own firm.   In Britain he had formed the
Gambia League and worked closely with nationalists of
other territories against continued British control of
African states.   In 1956, he and other educated Gambians formed the National Party which, however, ceased
to be a factor in politics by 1960.   In the latter 1950s,
he and his wife, Marion, published a small, informative Bathurst newspaper.   In the elections of 1962 and
1966, Foon associated himself with the United Party of
P. S. N'Jie.

FORDE, DR. ROBERT M.   Surgeon and medical researcher

who had previously served in the Gold Coast from 1891
to 1895. He was appointed to be Colonial Surgeon in
the Gambia in 1895 and became Senior Medical Officer
in 1904. In April 1901, he discovered in the blood of
a European patient a trypanosome, carried by the tsetse
fly, that was the cause of "sleeping sickness." Forde's
discovery of the Trypanosome gambiense was the first
major breakthrough in the treatment of this deadly disease whose cause had previously been a mystery.

FORO. The title given to a caste in Mandingo society. They
are freeborn members of a lineage comparable to the
Wolof badolo.

FORSTER, SAMUEL JOHN. Lawyer born in Bathurst in
1912 and educated at the Methodist Boys High School,
Fourah Bay College, and the Middle Temple in London.
He was a Colonial Magistrate in the Gambia from 1947-
53 and was the Liaison Officer in charge of the Gam-
bia Office in London from 1959-62. Forster moved to
Sierra Leone in 1963 when he was appointed a Police
Magistrate, a position he held until created a Pusine
Judge in 1966.

FORSTER, SMITH AND COMPANY. One of the oldest
British trading firms in the Gambia, it was operative
from the early 1820s. After the death of Matthew
Forster, the senior partner, the firm's business was
drastically reduced and its assets transferred in 1870
to another British firm of Lintott, Spink and Company.

FULBE (Fulani, Peul, Fula). A pastoral people whose home-
land was in the vicinity of the upper Senegal River and
who speak a variant of the Niger-Kordofanian language
family. They were the dominant group in the ancient
kingdom of Tekrur. After the overthrow of Tekrur,
the Fulbe created a series of smaller states from the
western segment of that state where they continued in
power until the Tucolor majority in those areas seized
power and established a strict Muslim rule in the Futa
Toro. Between the 13th and 18th centuries, large
numbers of Fulbe in a series of long, complicated migrations, established themselves throughout the western
and central Sudan as far eastward as the Cameroons.
They were an important element in the population of
Macina, were the base population for the theocracies
of the Futa Jallon, and were present in large numbers

in the Hausa states of northern Nigeria.  Usuman dan
Fodio, himself a Fulbe of Gobir, used them in the
early 19th century as the cadre for his jihad which
overran the Hausa states and created an empire in
northern Nigeria.  The Fulbe were present in large
numbers in the upper Gambia region in the 19th century where, although living in Mandingo states, they
maintained close ties with both the Futa Toro and Futa
Jallon.  Alfa Molloh in his revolt of the 1860s used
the Fulbe to create his kingdom of Fuladu.

FULBE BURURE.  A dialect group of the Fulbe who in the
latter 19th century migrated through Fuladu in great
numbers and were the principal owners of cattle in
the area in the 1870s.  They participated in the Fulbe
revolt against the Mandingo, but refused to serve Alfa
Molloh whose antecedents they held to be less pure
than their own.  Many of the Burure left Fuladu in the
1880s after their leaders quarrelled with Alfa Molloh.

FULBE FIRDU.  A dialect group of the Fulbe which today
number over 30,000 in the upper Gambia River area.
In the late 18th and early 19th centuries, they had
migrated in great numbers into the old Mandingo kingdoms of Tomani and Jimara.  They were semi-seden-
tary, normally spending 15 or more years in one location, and they tended to intermarry with other peoples in that locale.  The Fulbe Firdu comprised the
main support group for Alfa Molloh's rebellion against
his Mandingo overlords.

FULBE FUTO.  A dialect group of the Fulbe originally from
the Futa Jallon region.  In the latter 19th century they
settled in the southern section of Fuladu in what is now
the Casamance.  Before the Fulbe uprising of the 1860s,
groups of the Fulbe Futo continually raided into the
riverine areas.  Others of this group had temporarily
settled near the river to plant peanuts.  In the early
years of his ascendency, Alfa Molloh paid tribute to
the head of the Fulbe Futo in the Futa Jallon.

FUTA JALLON.  A highland area in what is now Guinea
with elevations up to 5000 feet.  It is also the source
of the Gambia, Senegal, and Niger Rivers.  In the
early 18th century, Fulbe reformers created there a
theocracy with the state controlled by elected almamis.
The Futa Jallon experience acted as a model for Islamic

reformers in the Futa Toro, northern Nigeria, and the
Gambia. Many Fulbe from the Futa Jallon regularly
migrated to the area which would later become southern
Fuladu. These Fulbe Futo became an important factor
in the success of Alfa Molloh, and the Almamy of Futa
Jallon loaned him fighting men to oppose the Mandingo
traditional rulers. The state of Futa Jallon remained
independent until the Almamy placed it under French
protection in 1888.

FUTA TORO. An area adjacent to the middle Senegal River
inhabited largely by Tucolor and Fulbe people. In
1776, a new theocratic state was created in the Futa
Toro led by Marabouts of the Qadiriyya tariq. Later
in the 19th century it became the centrum of the empire established by the Tijaniyya leader Al Hajj Umar
Tall. The Futa Toro acted as a training ground for
most of the Marabouts who wanted to convert the
"pagan" peoples of the Senegambia region. In addition,
the rulers of Futa Toro gave direct military assistance
to some of the war chiefs of the Gambia during the
Soninke-Marabout Wars.


-G-

GNP   see  GAMBIA NATIONAL PARTY

GNU   see  GAMBIA NATIONAL UNION

GPMB  see  GAMBIA PRODUCE MARKETING BOARD

GWU   see  GAMBIA WORKERS' UNION

GAMBIA ADVENTURERS. A joint stock company which was
allowed by the Royal Adventurers in 1668 to assume
the monopoly of trade in the areas adjacent to the
Gambia River. In 1684 after little profit and much
litigation in London, the Gambia Adventurers and their
parent company relinquished their trading monopoly to
the Royal African Company.

GAMBIA LABOUR UNION. A Bathurst-based general union
organized by Edward Small in 1929. In that year the
union called the first strike in Gambian history and
Small was successful in negotiating higher salaries for
artisans and river craft workers. Despite this minor

initial success the union was a very weak vehicle for protest during its entire existence. This was due to world economic conditions and the generally hostile attitude of the British authorities. The economic extension of Small's political activity and his position in the union helped him to be selected to the general executive council of the International Confederation of Free Trade Unions in 1932.

GAMBIA MINERALS COMPANY. British company formed to explore and exploit the ilmenite deposits near Brufut in 1954. Ilmenite ore, the source of rutile and titanium oxide, was in short supply, and the major producers in India had raised prices on the ore. Gambian deposits were found to be marginal, but construction began, nevertheless, in 1956 on a railroad, electric dry mill, and other facilities. Although the company invested over one million pounds, the entire operation was closed down in 1959 ostensibly because the world price of rutile had fallen to the point where it was unprofitable to continue operation.

GAMBIA NATIONAL PARTY (GNP). A Colony oriented party formed by a small number of educated Bathurst citizens in 1956. It was most effective in the various deliberations which led to the revision of the Constitution prior to the 1960 elections. The party never had a popular base of support and broke apart because of internal dissentions on the eve of the 1960 elections.

GAMBIA NATIONAL UNION (GNU). A small Colony based political party formed in 1961 to present alternatives to both the United Party and the People's Progressive Party. However, in the elections of 1962 and for some time afterward, it cooperated with the United Party. The Gambia National Union was never large, and by 1965, most of its members had either joined the United Party or had ceased to be active. By 1967, with the retirement of some key leaders, the party had ceased to function.

GAMBIA PRODUCE MARKETING BOARD (GPMB). Previously called the Gambia Oilseeds Marketing Board, it was created by the British colonial regime in 1949 to act as the chief purchasing agent for the peanut crop. The appointive board establishes a fixed payment per unit of decorticated and undecorticated nuts

and all peanut by-products based upon the previous
years experience.  GPMB has always followed the
practice of paying immediately the bulk of the purchase
price to the farmers.  Senegal, by contrast, for many
years paid higher prices, but on a three-payment system.  A large portion of the Sine and Saloum crop was
brought to the Gambia for the immediate payment.  The
name of the board was changed in 1971 when it became
necessary for the government to fund and purchase the
ever increasing Gambian rice crop as well as the peanut crop.

GAMBIA REGIMENT.  In 1901, the British recruited and
trained a unit of company strength which formed a part
of the Sierra Leone Battalion of the Royal West African Frontier Force.  During World War I, the Gambia
Company saw active service in Cameroon and East
Africa.  In 1939, the company was stationed in Sierra
Leone, but in the following year was posted to Bathurst
where it served as the cadre for the First Battalion of
the Gambia Regiment.  In 1941, the Second Battalion
was formed.  The First Battalion in 1943 was attached
to the Sixth Brigade of the 81st (West Africa) Division
in Nigeria.  From there, the division was moved to
the Far East, and the Battalion took part in the eight
day defense of Frontier Hill in Burma.  The Second
Battalion was also sent to the Far East and attached to
the 81st Division.  It took part in the victory at Myo-
haung and in the liberation of Rangoon.  Both units
returned to the Gambia in 1945, and after demobiliza-
tion, select elements were combined to form once again
the Gambia Company of the Sierra Leone Battalion.  In
1950, "A" Company became a separate entity and was
presented with its colors in April 1951, the only unit
of company strength to have them.  The Company
was broken up for financial reasons on the recommendation of Governor Wyn Harris, and a portion of the
soldiers were regrouped in 1958 as the Field Force, a
specialized unit of the police force.

GAMBIA WORKERS UNION (GWU).  The key labor organization in the Gambia.  It was formed in 1957 by M. E.
Jallow and some associates, and within a short period
had become an effective representative for many of the
workers in Bathurst and at the peanut shipping ports
of Kaur and Kuntaur.  In 1961, the British authorities
charged that Jallow in the course of a strike of dock

workers had incited them to violence. Although found
guilty, he was given only a nominal fine, and his
union was successful in gaining many of its demands
from the government. The Gambia Workers Union
stood aloof from direct participation in the elections
of 1960 and 1962, but it appeared that by 1964 Jallow
was prepared to use the union in a more open political
manner. However, he accepted the position of Secretary General with the African Regional Office of the
International Confederation of Free Trade Unions in
that year. Without him the union withdrew from overt
political activity in the latter 1960s, and its leaders
became concerned only with the problems of labor.

GARBA-JAHUMPA, IBRIMAH MOMODOU. Teacher, labor
    leader, and politician, born in Bathurst in 1912 of a
    family which had migrated from Senegal in 1816. He
    attended Koranic school, primary, and secondary
    schools in Bathurst, and completed work at the Teachers
    Training College in 1936. He became a teacher and
    taught until 1949 in Bathurst and Georgetown except for
    a brief period during World War II when he was asso-
    ciated with BOAC. He was Secretary of the Gambia
    Labor Union from 1939 to 1945 and was a member of
    the International Confederation of Free Trade Unions.
    Garba-Jahumpa's political activities began in 1935 when
    he became Assistant Secretary of the Bathurst Rate
    Payers Association. He was appointed a member of
    the Bathurst Town Council in 1942, was elected a mem-
    ber in 1947, and in 1959 became the first Chairman of
    the Council. He won one of the two elected seats to
    the Legislative Council in the elections of 1951, and
    three months after the election was instrumental in
    coalescing a number of Muslim organizations into the
    Muslim Congress Party. Garba-Jahumpa was re-
    elected in 1954 and was appointed Minister of Agri-
    culture and Natural Resources, a post he held until
    the elections of 1960. Two months before that election,
    the Muslim Congress merged with the Democratic Party
    to form the Democratic Congress Alliance. However,
    this coalition was not successful since it elected only
    one member from the Colony area. In 1961, an agree-
    ment was reached with the People's Progressive Party
    whereby in future elections, no PPP candidate would
    stand against a DCA sponsored candidate. Despite this,
    the DCA in 1962 returned only one member to the House
    of Assembly, and Garba-Jahumpa was defeated by a

United Party candidate.  Soon afterward, Garba-Jahumpa broke with the DCA and organized the Congress
Party.  With this as a vehicle, Garba-Jahumpa was
elected to the House of Assembly in 1964.  By 1968,
he had resolved his differences with the PPP through
compromise.  The Congress Party was disbanded and
Garba-Jahumpa became Minister of Health and Social
Welfare.  In early 1973, he was appointed Minister of
Finance.

GARRISON SCHOOL.  The school created by the British for
the education and training of African soldiers stationed
in the Gambia.  The school at Bathurst was particularly important during Governor D'Arcy's tenure in
producing a small number of competent African non-
commissioned officers.

GEREGIA.  The site of a Portuguese settlement on the south
bank of the Bintang Bolon approximately twenty miles
from the village of Bintang.  It is conjectured that the
present-day village of Kansala is near the site of Geregia.  In the 1650s the area near Geregia was a favorite
trading locale for the English.  They established a
factory there as early as 1689 and continued to maintain trading posts there throughout the early 18th century.

GEWEL.  A Wolof term for persons whose responsibilities
were to act as musicians and praise singers.  Called
griots by the French, they were one section of the low
born caste called nenyo.

GOLBERY, S. M. X.  An official of the French trading
company in the Senegambia during the mid-1780s.  In
1802 he published a two-volume account of his experiences entitled Fragments d'un voyage en Afrique.

GOMEZ, DIEGO.  A one-time page to Prince Henry of Portugal, he led an expedition which entered the Gambia
estuary in 1457.  Gomes met with chiefs who the year
before had received Cadamosto, travelled upriver to
Kantora, and traded for considerable gold.  His reports
of the rich gold fields of the interior combined with the
gold he brought back helped convince Europe of the
wealth to be had in interior trade.  Gomes' reports
also led to the first two Portuguese missionaries being
sent to the Gambia in an abortive attempt to convert the
riverine Africans.

GOULDSBURY, VALESIUS S. (Surgeon-Major). Administrator of the Gambia from 1877 until 1884. In 1880, the Governor in Chief, Sir Samuel Rowe, proposed that part of the £19,000 surplus in the Gambian treasury be used to finance an expedition into the hinterland as far as the Futa Jallon with the purpose of investigating trading possibilities and entering into friendly relations with African rulers. When this was approved, Administrator Gouldsbury was chosen to lead the exploration. In 1881, Gouldsbury followed the path laid down by his instructions and proceeded as far as the Futa Jallon. He made a number of treaties with the rulers of the upper river and the Futa Jallon. The expedition was valuable only because it gave the government up-to-date information on the events then transpiring in the interior and because it confirmed what Lieutenant-Governor MacDonnell had said in 1849 about the paucity of trading opportunities there. Gouldsbury believed that any profits to be made there would be more than offset by the expense involved. His negative report helped support the general British attitude that the interior lands were worthless and predisposed the Colonial Office to adopt a quiescent attitude toward French expansion into the interior during the 1880s.

GRANT, ALEXANDER (Captain; later Lieutenant Colonel). Captain Grant was sent from Goree in March 1816 with two officers, 50 men of the African Corps, and 24 artisans with orders to reoccupy Fort James, in order to protect British trade rights to the Gambia and to check the trade in slaves. Grant arranged with the ruler of Barra for the reoccupation by agreeing to pay approximately £75 per year. He soon discovered that the fort was almost beyond repair and suggested to his superiors that Banjul be occupied instead. Colonel Brereton with 30 more men joined Grant in April and together they negotiated with the king of Kombo the cession of the island for a payment of approximately £25 per year. On April 23, 1816, Grant took formal possession of the island and began work on barracks and gun emplacements. The king of Barra allowed the British to take stone from Dog Island for their construction work. The British at Goree advertised special privileges for merchants who established themselves at the new settlement called Bathurst. By early 1819, there were 700 civilians in the town and within a decade, over 1800. Grant was responsible for laying

out the basic pattern of the city of Bathurst with its
streets named after Waterloo generals.  He built
the earliest section of Government House, and the barracks he constructed were long used as government
offices.  Grant took the lead role in urging merchants
towards legitimate trade, and from the beginning used
all the forces at his command to stop the riverine
slave trade.  He also encouraged the missionary activities of the Society of Friends and the Wesleyans.
In 1823, he negotiated the occupation of the island of
Lemaine (renamed MacCarthy) and ordered the construction of a mud fort, called Fort George, which was
then manned by a dozen soldiers.  Grant also served
as Acting Governor of Sierra Leone in 1820 and again
in 1821.  He was promoted to Major in the second
West India Regiment just before he turned over command of the Gambia garrison to Captain Findley in
1823.

GRAY, SIR JOHN M.  A Justice in the High Court of the
Gambia in the 1930s.  He is most remembered for his
long, detailed, scholarly work, A History of the Gambia, published in 1940.  It has remained the standard
work on Gambian history through the 19th century.

GRIOT  see  GEWEL

GRIS-GRIS.  Charms which the wearer believes have the
power to either ward off a specific evil or to enable
him to perform certain tasks.  These were originally
in traditional society compounded by someone who was
believed to have unique powers in communicating with
the spirit world.  Today many Muslims wear small
leather-bound verses of the Koran which they have received from a Marabout.

GROUNDNUTS.  A spreading, hairy, annual leguminous herb
(Archis hypogasa) which provides the main cash crop
of Gambian farmers.  The plant is native to Brazil and
was brought to Europe in the 16th century from where
it was taken to all parts of the world.  The groundnut,
or peanut, was introduced to the Gambia by the Portuguese and was noted by such early English visitors as
Jobson and Moore.  However, its cultivation as a cash
crop did not begin until the great increase in demand
for fats and oils which occurred in Europe in the last
75 years of the 19th century.  The first shipment of

peanuts from the Gambia was in 1830, worth only
slightly more than £10.  By 1890, over 18,000 tons
worth £130,000 were exported.  In the 1960s, the annual crop of the Gambia was over 100,000 tons.  Peanuts are planted in April or May just before the rainy
season.  The Mandinka and Jola plant the peanuts in
ridges while the Wolof plant them on the flat.  Weeding
is a continuous process during the growing season.
Harvesting is normally done by digging the plants by
hand, generally during October.  The plants are then
stacked to dry, and threshing is done after the trading
season opens in December.  The nuts are then sacked
and transported to the buying stations.

GUELOWAR.   The title of the matrilineage from which the
rulers of Sine and Saloum were chosen.   This matrilineage was historically that which had led a northward
moving Mandingo migration which in the 13th or 14th
centuries encountered the southward migrating Serer.
It is from this meeting that the complex political institutions of the Serer states can be dated.

GUINEA COMPANY (British).   Formed in 1651 by the Commonwealth in expectation of riches to be gained from
West African trade.   Two trading expeditions were sent
to Gambia, a factory established on Bintang Bolon, and
traders sent as far into the interior as Barrakunda.   A
series of accidents destroyed much of the trade goods,
large numbers of the Europeans were incapacitated by
illness and many died, and finally in early 1652, Prince
Rupert and a small royalist fleet entered the Gambia
River and seized the company ships.   Following this
disaster, the Commonwealth abandoned all attempts to
trade in the Gambia.

GUM TRADE.   Established in the 16th century, the trade in
gum arabic (derived from the Acacia arabica tree) had
by the 18th century become very important for some
West African traders.   The Royal African Company began to trade for this item at the station of Portendic in
Mauritania.   Both French and British gum merchants
suffered because of the European wars of the 18th century.   One of Governor Faidherbe's first goals in the
1850s was to end the exclusive power of the Mauritanian sheikhs over this trade.   Soon afterward in 1857,
Britain relinquished its rights to the trade at Portendic
in return for French abandonment of their station of Albreda on the Gambia River.

GUNJUR. A town in southern Kombo which was the main
base of operations of the young Marabout Fodi Kabba
in the 1850s who in collaboration with Omar of Sabaji
almost defeated the British forces in Bathurst. It continued to be a Marabout stronghold during the 1860s
and was a particularly important base during the final
conquest of the Soninkes in Kombo during the 1870s.
Fodi Silla had by this time come to control Gunjur and
his activities against the Boundary Commission finally
brought a British punitive expedition into Kombo. Gun-
jar and Fodi Silla's other main towns were taken in
1894, and he was forced to flee to the Casamance
where he was captured by the French.

-H-

HALF DIE. A portion of Banjul (Bathurst) adjacent to Jolof
Town at the lower end of Wellington Street and bordered
on one side by the Atlantic Ocean and on another by the
Gambia River. This area, also called Moka Town,
was inhabited by the poorer residents of the city. Until protective measures were taken in the 20th century,
Half Die was nothing but a sandbank in the dry season
and a swamp during the rains. Ostensibly the section
received its name because of the high mortality rate
there in the 19th century.

HANNO. Carthaginian soldier and mariner who in about
500 B.C. was commissioned to investigate the western
coastline of Africa. According to writing on a stone
column at the Temple of Baal in Carthage, Hanno's
ships reached the Chertes (Senegal) River and then the
Bambotus, "a large and broad river" full of crocodiles
and hippopotami. This latter river was probably the
Gambia. H. Richmond Palmer in The Carthaginian
Voyage to West Africa comments that Hanno probably
reached the vicinity of Sierra Leone before turning
back.

HAVELOCK, SIR ARTHUR E. Governor of the West African
Settlements (Sierra Leone and the Gambia) from 1881
to 1884. He was a delegate to the 1881 Commission to
deal with the French over the Sierra Leone boundary.
The question of a generalized exchange of territory including the Gambia by both powers was discussed, but
the British refused to consider ceding the Gambia at
that time.

HELM, HENRY (HEINRICH). A Prussian born and naturalized British citizen and resident of Bathurst who was responsible after 1870 for managing the Gambian affairs of Thomas Chown and Sons. He became a member of the Legislative Council in 1878 and continued the Chowns' opposition to any cession of the Gambia to France.

HEMMING, AUGUSTUS. A senior British civil servant in the Colonial Office and an expert on West African affairs. He was one of the two British delegates to the Paris Conference which produced the Convention of 1889 that drew the boundaries of the Gambia.

HODGES, SAMUEL. A soldier in the 4th West India Regiment stationed in the Gambia in 1866 to support Colonel D'Arcy's attack upon Amer Faal's stronghold of Tubab Kolon. On July 26, artillery fire having proved to have little effect on the stockade, D'Arcy called for volunteers to advance under fire and chop a hole in the wooden walls with axes. Hodges was one of the 17 men who volunteered. Only he and another soldier named Boswell reached the wall, and they began to hew away while the defenders concentrated a heavy fire on them. Boswell was killed, but Hodges continued his work and made a hole in the wall. D'Arcy then led his men through the gap, following Hodges who also breached two of the inner walls with his axe. For this display of conspicious bravery, Hodges was awarded the Victoria Cross.

HOLMES, MAJOR ROBERT. Appointed in 1661 as commander of a small fleet of ships outfitted by the Royal Adventurers of England Trading into Africa to establish their dominance on the Gambia River. He occupied Dog Island, cultivated the friendship of the ruler of Kombo, and finally forced the surrender of the Courlanders on St. Andrew's Island. Holmes renamed the island after James, the Duke of York. Although Holmes' action against the Courlanders was unauthorized, English possession of the Courlander's fort and trading stations was used to force the cession of the Courlander rights to the English in 1664. In 1663, Holmes was again sent with two ships to the Gambia to unload stores and ascertain the situation of the garrison he had left. Upon being informed of the presence of a hostile Dutch ship in Gambian waters, Holmes took his three ships northward and captured the Dutch trading entrepôt of Goree. His actions

had a precipitating effect on the second English-Dutch
conflict, for the States General dispatched Admiral de
Ruyter and 13 ships to recapture Goree. Although de
Ruyter by-passed James Island, this victory was one of
the first in the second trade war between the two great
maritime powers.

HORTON, DR. JAMES AFRICANUS. Medical officer, writer,
and businessman, born in Gloucester, Sierra Leone in
1835. He attended village schools, the Church Missionary Grammar School, and Fourah Bay College. He
was one of three Africans selected by the British in
1855 for medical training. In 1858 he completed work
at Kings College, London, and was admitted to the
Royal College of Surgeons. He later completed his
doctorate at Edinburgh in 1859 and entered the army as
a staff assistant-surgeon the same year and was posted
to the Gold Coast. He took part in the Ashanti War of
1864 and was sent to the Gambia the following year.
He accompanied the British troops sent to MacCarthy
Island to counter the threats to British hegemony there.
After the soldiers were withdrawn, Horton stayed behind as commandant, entered into friendly relations
with neighboring chiefs, and helped organize a pro-
visional government for the island. When the regular
British magistrate arrived in June 1866, Horton left
and arrived in Bathurst in time to give his professional
aid during the yellow fever epidemic. In 1867, he returned to the Gold Coast. Until his death in 1883, he
continued to be a spokesman for the Africans.

HOUGHTON, MAJOR DONALD. A British army officer and
explorer. He was stationed at Goree in 1780 when
ordered to Bintang with 80 men and four small ships
to cut timber. While there he was forced by a French
man-of-war to sink his ships and take refuge with the
Jola. Aided by them, Houghton managed to drive off
the French landing parties and was later rescued by a
British warship. In 1790, Houghton was chosen by the
Association for Promoting the Discovery of the Interior
Parts of Africa to try to open communications between
the Gambia and Timbuktu. He travelled to Medina near
Barrakunda Falls and from there proceeded to Bambuk
where he either died of disease or was murdered.

HUNGRY SEASON. Concentration on groundnuts (peanuts),
the one cash crop of the Gambia, poor roads, and a

faulty system of distribution of local surpluses of foods
led to chronic food shortages by the early 1930s for a
portion of the year just before harvest time.  In some
of the upper river areas near famine conditions pre-
vailed during this "hungry season."  To offset this, the
Colonial government had to import large quantities of
rice, usually of an inferior quality, which was dis-
tributed to the people.  Beginning in the 1950s, more
farmers were induced to plant rice, fertilizers were
used, ox-plowing schools were started, and foreign
rice experts were brought to the Protectorate.  This
concentration on rice production, coupled with more
improved market facilities and all-weather roads, has
ended the hungry season which was once such an accepted part of the lives of so many Gambians.

HUNTLEY, SIR HENRY VERE.  Lieutenant-Governor of the
Gambia in 1840, succeeding William Mackie who had
governed for only six months.  Huntley found the Colony
in debt, the problems of the liberated Africans still un-
solved, and British prestige in the upper river at a
very low level.  Huntley provided space for the resettlement of liberated Africans by convincing Suling Jata,
the ruler of Kombo, to cede to the Crown the district
now known as Kombo St. Mary.  In the MacCarthy
Island area there was a brief period of violence between various factions during which the chief of Nyani-
bantang was killed.  After Huntley ordered the British
there to maintain strict neutrality between feuding factions and denied the island as a place of sanctuary,
British prestige was soon restored.  He reinforced the
garrison at MacCarthy Island, gained the cession of
land for a small fort at Kataba, and entered into a
treaty of protection with the chief.  This latter treaty,
however, was disavowed by the Colonial Office.  In
1842, Huntley was transferred to Prince Edward Island.

HUTTON, WILLIAM.  Administrator temporarily in charge
of the British administration at Bathurst in 1829.  Without consulting the Colonial Office, he had induced
Bathurst merchants to subscribe some £7,000 of goods
for interior trade, contingent upon satisfactory treaties
with hinterland chiefs.  In April and May of 1829, he
entered into agreements which would allow the British
to build factories at Kantalikunda, and the king of Wuli
ceded Fattatenda outright.  Hutton's agreements were
repudiated by the British government and he was later

dismissed from the service because of questions over
his handling of public finance.

-I-

IBRAHIMA, ALFA.  One of the powerful Fulbe rulers of the
Futa Jallon in the late 19th century who played an important role in the success of Alfa Molloh in his wars
against the traditional Mandingo rulers of Jimara, Tomani, and Eropina.  In the late 1860s, he sent his son
with Fulbe reinforcements to aid Alfa Molloh's armies,
and continued to support the Fulbe throughout the 1870s.
In 1879, large numbers of Ibrahima's troops took part
in the campaign against Simotto Moro at Tubakuta.  Although Alfa Molloh did not consider himself subject to
Ibrahima, there was a positive client relationship between Fuladu and the Futa Jallon.

ILER.  The name of a tool with a short handle and an in-
verted, heart-shaped blade used in cultivation by Wolof
and Mandingo peanut farmers in Saloum and the Gambia.  The iler is the main tool used to clear weeds
and also to loosen the soil around the plants at harvest
time.

ILMENITE.  A mineral which is the source of rutile, titanium oxide, and zircon.  It is found in marginal quantities in the Gambia.  Between 1956 and 1959, the
Gambia Minerals Company operated a mine and plant
near Brufut for processing ilmenite.  Mining operations
ceased because of a fall in the world market price of
rutile and zircon.

INDIRECT RULE.  The term which describes the general
administrative policy followed by Great Britain in
governing the bulk of its African territories.  In theory,
African traditional rulers, with the supervision of European District Officers, would be authorized to continue
to make the basic administrative and legal decisions for
their people.  In the Gambia this was complicated because the Soninke-Marabout Wars had disturbed and in
some cases destroyed the older kingdoms and their
ruling classes.  The first attempt at Indirect Rule came
with the appointment of Travelling Commissioners in
1893 and the Protectorate Ordinance of 1894.  Subsequent Ordinances had created by 1945 a system whereby

the bulk of the Gambia was governed by 35 appointed
chiefs. Legislation sponsored by Governors Palmer
and Richards from 1933 to 1935 brought the theory and
practice of government in line with the concepts of
Lugard and Sir Donald Cameron. A Senior Commissioner to provide continuity of policy and centralization
of planning was appointed in 1944. In the same year
the government established the annual Conference of
Protectorate Chiefs.

ISMAIL, AL HAJJ. A Mauritanian teacher who in the early
1850s travelled through the western Sudan preaching a
jihad against the infidel. He probably never visited
the Gambia, but one of his agents, Omar, took up residence in Sabaji where he, in conjunction with the Marabouts of Gunjur, planned the attack in 1855 upon the
Soninkes of Kombo which almost succeeded in taking
Bathurst. Shortly afterward, Ismail was captured by
the French and sent into exile to Cayenne.


-J-


JACK, ALIEU SULAYMAN. Civil servant and politician,
born at Bathurst in 1922 into a Muslim Wolof family.
He was educated at the Roman Catholic mission school
and joined the Civil Service during World War II. In
1950, he began his political career when elected to the
Bathurst Town Council. He early associated himself
with the People's Progressive Party and became the
Speaker of the House of Assembly after the elections
of 1962. In the government reorganization following
the Republic plebiscite, he was named Minister for
Works and Communications.

JALLOW, MOMADOU EBRIMA. A Gambian labor leader,
born in Georgetown in June 1928 and educated through
the secondary level at St. Augustine's School. He
joined the Civil Service as a clerk in the Education
Department and later in the Income Tax Division. He
also worked in the mid-1950s as a secretary-accountant
for private firms in Bathurst. At the urging of friends,
he formed the Gambia Construction Employees Society
which led to the creation in late 1957 of the Gambia
Workers Union. Although with little experience of
unionism, Jallow was able in 1958 to negotiate a number
of favorable contracts with employers. In late 1958 he

attended a four-month course in trade unionism at Kam-
pala and began to make contacts outside the Gambia.
Throughout 1959 he concentrated on building union
strength among the dock workers and daily paid employees.   The following year, at the height of the peanut season, his union conducted the first successful
large-scale strike in the Gambia.   This strike gained
a substantial increase in the wages of daily workers
and eventually led to the formation of Joint Industrial
Councils for the arbitration of labor disputes.   The
British government decision to indict him for taking
part in a riot merely increased his popularity among
Gambians.   Jallow's decision not to enter politics at
this period in Gambian history was crucial since his
popularity might have created a political vehicle which
could have challenged the older parties.   In 1964, Jallow became the full time Secretary-General of the
African Regional Office of the International Confederation of Free Trade Unions with headquarters at Lagos.

JAM.   A Wolof word for non-freeborn persons.   Slaves in
Wolof society belonged to one of two groups--those born
in captivity and those captured in war.   Although some
slaves held high positions and most were treated well,
they were always considered to be the property of the
master who could do with them what he wished.

JAMBUR.   A title in Wolof areas denoting freeborn persons.   The freeborn were divided into three cate-
gories--those belonging to royal lineages, nobles not
of such lineages, and the badolo or peasants who
made up the bulk of the population in a Wolof
state.

JARRA.   One of the nine Mandingo kingdoms located along
the south bank of the Gambia River in the early 19th
century.   It joined Kiang on the west and extended eastward to Sofancama Bolon.   During the latter stages of
the Soninke-Marabout Wars much of Jarra was controlled by the powerful Marabout leader, Fodi Kabba.
Because of the antipathy between Fodi Kabba and Musa
Molloh, the area of eastern Jarra became a particular
arena of conflict.   In the 20th-century reorganization
of the Protectorate, Jarra became a part of the Central
Division and was divided into three districts, each under
the direction of a chief.

JATTA, SULING. The king of Kombo who in 1840 was pressured by Lieutenant-Governor Huntley to cede to Britain
a part of his kingdom for the payment of $100 which
afterward became known as British Kombo or Kombo St.
Mary. This area was enlarged by a later cession in
1853 and gave the British approximately twenty-five
square miles of land adjoining St. Mary's Island.
Suling Jatta renounced his right to collect customs duties and rents in the ceded territory in 1850 in consideration of a small annual payment. His kingdom
was one of the first Gambian areas to be struck by
Islamic proselytizers. These Marabouts were particularly strong in Gunjur and Sabaji (Sukuta). By the end
of 1851, it was apparent that Suling Jatta was losing
much of his support to the preaching and raiding of the
Muslims. Governor MacDonnell tried to persuade the
Colonial Office to take much of Kombo under British
protection and thus bring an end to the internecine
struggle. He was only authorized to seek a cession of
a small strip of land from the king to add to British
Kombo. This included the town of Sabaji, most of
whose elders were Soninke, but the bulk of the population was loyal to the Marabouts. After much consideration, Suling Jatta agreed to the cession in May 1853.
The townspeople of Sabaji refused to accept the agreement, and British forces took the town by storm in
1853. This was not the end of the affair since the
Marabout leaders, Omar and Fodi Kabba, launched an
attack in June 1855 against both Suling Jatta and British
Kombo. The Marabouts almost succeeded in taking
Bathurst. Marabouts from Gunjur tried to take Busumballa, the king's town. The attack was beaten off, but
Suling Jatta was killed. The ensuing struggle for power
between the Soninke families of Yundum and Busumballa
over the succession greatly helped the Kombo Marabouts
in their bid for power.

JAWARA. The title given to a general appointed to command
the armies in a Mandingo state.

JAWARA, SIR DAUDA KAIRABA. Prime Minister of the Gambia from 1962 to 1970 and President of the Republic
since its inception in 1970. He was born in the Protectorate at Barajally in 1924. His father, a prosperous
Mandinka farmer, chose him from among his six sons
to be educated at Bathurst, first at the Muslim primary
school, then later at the Methodist Boys High School.

After graduation in 1945, he worked at the Royal Victoria Hospital and won a scholarship to Achimota College and later attended the Veterinary School at Glas-
gow University where he qualified as a veterinary
surgeon.   In the 1950s, he gained a further diploma
in tropical veterinary medicine.   In 1954, he returned
to the Gambia and became a veterinary officer in the
Protectorate.   In 1955, he was converted to Christianity
and married Augusta, a daughter of Sir John Mahoney,
one of the leaders of the Aku community in Bathurst.
They had five children before their divorce in 1967.
He subsequently married the present Lady Jawara.   In
1965, Jawara reverted to Islam and changed his name
from David to Dauda.   He helped form the People's
Progressive Party in 1959 and was chosen its leader.
In the elections of 1960, the PPP elected nine representatives to the House as compared to the opposition
United Party's seven, and Jawara served briefly as
Minister of Education.   However, he and all the PPP
ministers resigned when the governor appointed P. S.
N'Jie of the United Party as Chief Minister.   In the
elections of 1962, Jawara's party won an overwhelming
victory and he became Prime Minister.   His government cooperated fully with the governor and the Colonial Office in negotiating the constitutional instruments
of an independent Gambia.   When the Gambia became
independent on February 18, 1965, Jawara continued as
Prime Minister.   As such, he was responsible for the
increasing solvency of the government and for continuing
an evolutionary program of closer cooperation with
Senegal.   He was knighted in 1966.   Jawara's proposal
to convert the Gambia to a Republic was rejected by the
voters in 1965 by only 700 votes.   However, when resubmitted to the electorate in April 1970, the change
was overwhelmingly approved.   On April 24, Jawara
became the first President of the Republic of the Gambia.

JIMARA.   One of the nine Mandingo kingdoms located along
the south bank of the Gambia River in the early 19th
century.   It was one of the larger and more prosperous
of the upriver polities and had a long history of trade
with Europeans since MacCarthy Island was located adjacent to the middle areas of Jimara.   Alfa Molloh was
a resident of Jimara and it was there that he made his
first conquest, overthrowing the traditional Mandingo
dynasty.   Jimara became the nucleus of his new kingdom

of Fuladu.  In the 20th century reorganization of the
chiefdoms, the area which was Jimara became the Districts of Fuladu West and Fuladu Central.

JOAR.  A village on the north bank of the mid-Gambia River
which was the site of a number of trade factories established by the Portuguese and later English trading
companies.  The English had factories there in 1704
and between 1723 and 1727.  The Royal African Company post there in the 1730s was their principal out
factory on the river.

JOB BEN SOLOMON (Job Jallow).  Son of a Fulbe ruler in
Bondu.  In the early 18th century he was captured in
the Gambia and sold into slavery.  Job was transported
to Maryland where he labored for over a year.  Fortunately, one of his letters, written to his father in
Arabic, fell into the hands of General Oglethorpe who
was so impressed that he ransomed him.  Job then
began a 14-month stay in Britain where he assisted Sir
Hans Sloane with Arabic translations and was presented
at the court of George II.  Agents of the Royal African
Company were ordered to treat him with great respect
when he returned to the Gambia in 1734.  He and
Francis Moore became good friends and Job accompanied Moore on a number of travels to trading stations
before returning to Bondu in 1736 with a company servant, Thomas Hull.  Job was responsible for inter-
ceding with one of his patrons, the Duke of Montagu,
to free a friend, Lahmin Jay, from slavery in Maryland.  Jay, after returning to Gambia, joined Job in
Bondu.  The last record of Job dates to 1740 when he
came to James Island and led a company agent, Mel-
chior de Jaspas, back to Bondu.

JOBSON, RICHARD.  A supercargo for the English Guinea
Company who arrived with two ships and much trade
goods in the Gambia in 1620.  After seizing property
from local Protuguese inhabitants in reprisal for their
looting and subsequent massacre of the crew of an
English ship, Jobson's ships proceded to Tendeba.
Jobson took one of the ships to Mangegar where a house
was purchased from the chief which was to be used as
a trading factory.  It was decided that Jobson with
seven men should continue the exploration of the river.
He reached Barrakunda Falls in January 1621, and
Tenda the following month.  He made friends with the

local rulers, discovered the nature and type of trade
to be had in the upper river, and found that the Portuguese were no longer a force on the river. By the
time that Jobson returned to his ships, disease had reduced the complement to such an extent that Jobson left
the Gambia in May. He was convinced of the wealth
which could be obtained by trading in the Gambia and
labored hard to convince the English Royal family to
subsidize further ventures. One of the propaganda
weapons he used was his book on the expedition entitled The Golden Trade. In 1624, he was entrusted
with command of another expedition to the Gambia but
the venture was a failure. A later book, The Discovery
of the Country of King Solomon, did not further influence English sponsors, but played an important role in
spurring French interest in the Senegambia. The
French formed a company in 1626 to exploit the river
trade. Jobson, however, never returned to the Gambia.

JOINER, THOMAS. A Mandinka merchant who, in the early
19th century, became one of the most affluent Bathurst
traders. He had been a griot as a young man, but
was captured and sold into slavery in one of the southern United States. There he learned the craft of car-
pentry (which probably gave him his name). He was
fortunate to be able to purchase his freedom and, in
about 1805, had returned to the Gambia. Beginning
with only a small amount of money, he had, by trading
with the upper river areas, become wealthy even before
the town of Bathurst was begun. Joiner owned a number of ships and boats engaged in the river trade among
which was the largest craft operating from the port of
Bathurst. His ships made regular journeys with passen-
gers and cargo to Sierra Leone, the Cape Verdes, the
Isles de Los, and the Madeiras. At one time he employed over 100 persons to help carry on his trading
activities. Joiner considered himself, and was so considered, a prominent member of the largely European
trading community of Senegambia. He had become by
the time of his death in 1842 the most respected Gambian trader in Bathurst.

JOKADU. One of the five Mandingo controlled kingdoms on
the north bank of the Gambia River in the early 19th
century, bounded on the west by Jurunku Bolon and on
the east by Kutang Bolon. In 1862, the area was captured by Amer Faal, one of Ma Bâ's lieutenants, and

the people were forced to accept Islam. It was then
incorporated into Ma Bâ's kingdom of Baddibu (Rip)
and its history in the latter years of the century was
bound to the struggles for control of this larger state
by the successors of Ma Bâ. The chieftancy was restored by the British reorganization of the Protectorate
in the 20th century when it became a District in the
Lower River Division.

JOLAS. Comprise approximately 10 per cent of the population of the Gambia with the majority (approximately
20,000) residing in the Foni areas south of Bintang
Bolon. Some Jola traditions suggest a common origin
for themselves and the Serer in the upper Gambia
region. They still maintain a joking relationship with
the Serer. It is probable that the Jolas are the people
longest resident in the Gambia region and were overcome by a series of Mandingo invasions. Some of the
earliest European visitors mention the Jola, whom they
called Feloops, living in the same locales where they
now live. Their political and social organization was
village oriented and not as sophisticated as those of the
Mandingo or Wolof. Moore and Park both reported in
the 18th century that although the Jola paid tribute to
their Mandingo overlords, they had not been completely
subjugated and continued to exercise great freedom.
The Jola were noted for their competence in war. A
number of times in the 18th century the Jola came to
the assistance of British traders and soldiers during
conflicts with the French. In the latter 19th century
many Jola served as mercenaries in the Soninke-Marabout Wars. Disdaining the religious position of both
Muslims and Mandingo, they served both sides. However, they strongly resisted the attempts by Fodi Kabba
to convert them to Islam. In 1887, the chiefs of 16
Jola towns signed a treaty with Sir Samuel Rowe at
Kansala whereby they placed themselves under British
protection.

JOLOF. The original of the Wolof states, it was formed
before the 14th century. Its rise was probably occa-
sioned by the breakup of the kingdom of Tekrur and
the demise of Malian power in the Senegambia region.
The Wolof probably migrated from Tekrur into most
parts of what is now Senegal. Eventually by the 16th
century, five major states--Walo, Cayor, Baol, Sine,
and Saloum--owed allegiance to the ruler (burba) of

Jolof. In the course of the following century all of
these revolted against Jolof domination and the state
became relatively isolated from the lucrative trade
with Europeans. Because of its location, it was open
to attacks from Mauritania and by the more prosperous
coastal states of Cayor, Walo, and Baol. Much of the
population was early converted to Islam. In the Soninke-Marabout Wars, Jolof was conquered by Ma Bâ's
forces and briefly became a part of the kingdom of
Rip. The Burba Jolof in the 1880s allied himself with
the faction supporting Saër Maty in Baddibu. The use
of Jolof for raids into French protected areas led to a
French expedition in 1890 and its subsequent absorption
into the French empire.

JOLOF TOWN. A section of Banjul (Bathurst) adjacent to
Soldier Town and Half Die fronting on Wellington Street,
and is sometimes called Melville Town. It is today
the site of most of the major trading and business establishments. In the early 19th century this section of
the city was largely inhabited by Wolof artisans.

JONES, SAMUEL H. M. Educator and government official,
born of an Aku family in Bathurst in 1923. He was
educated at the Bathurst Methodist Boys High School,
Achimota, Exeter University, and the London Institute
of Education. From 1944 to 1947, he taught in the
Gambian primary schools. In 1952, he became the assistant master of his old high school where he remained
until entering government service as an education officer
in 1960. In the 1950s he was the president of the Gambia Teachers Union and a representative on the West
African Examinations Council. He was seconded to the
World Confederation of Organizations of the Teaching
Profession in 1960, travelled extensively throughout
Africa, and produced a report for them on the status
of teaching in Africa. In 1962, he returned briefly to
the Gambian Ministry of Education before being posted
as Liaison Officer to the Gambia Office in London.
Later he became Commissioner when the name of the
office was changed.

JONES, SAMUEL HORTON OLUWALE. A medical practitioner,
born in 1909 and educated at the Methodist Boys High
School. In 1925, he transferred to the Church Missionary
Society Grammar School in Freetown and after completion
of work there in 1928, attended Manchester University,

receiving his degree in 1934. He then attended the
London School of Tropical Hygiene and Medicine and
became a Medical Officer in the Gambia in 1936. He
was promoted to Senior Medical Officer in 1951, and
became the Director of Medical Services in the following year, a post he held until retirement in 1964.

JONGO.   The title given in Mandingo society to the slaves,
comparable to the Wolof jam.

JUFFURE.   A Mandingo village on the north bank of the
Gambia River opposite James Island. In the early 18th
century there was also a large number of half-caste
Portuguese residents there. The English maintained
factories there for a century after 1680. At first
these were sponsored by the large chartered companies,
but later were maintained by independent traders. In
the early 18th century, Juffure provided the garrison at
Fort James with a large portion of their vegetable requirements.

JUNJUN.   A small drum approximately $2\frac{1}{2}$ feet long used by
the Wolof only to announce the arrival of chiefs. It is
beaten by a curved stick, only one hand being used by
the drummer.

JUSTOBAQUE, PETER.   The factor of the (Dutch) West Indies
Company at Goree who in mid-1661 attempted to oust
the British from their newly won superiority in trade on
the Gambia River. Sailing up the Gambia River, he
partly neutralized the small British garrison at Charles
Fort on Dog Island. However, he was thwarted by the
firm action of the British factor at James Fort who refused all Justobaque's arguments, promises of reward,
and threats. Finally, Justobaque withdrew from the
river and the directors of the Dutch company and the
States General took no further immediate action to drive
the English from the Gambia.

-K-

KABBA, FODI.   A Mandingo Muslim who as a young man
was partly responsible for the beginnings of the Soninke-
Marabout conflict in Kombo. With his power base at
Gunjur, he collaborated with the inhabitants of Sabaji to
attack the Soninke king of Kombo in 1855. The governor,

Colonel O'Connor, responded with troops and the British
sustained extremely heavy losses in June of that year.
Although convinced that Fodi Kabba was primarily responsible for the attack, O'Connor could not retaliate
against him because of the depletion of his force and he
arranged peace between the Marabouts and Soninkes in
the Kombo in April 1856. In the next decade, Fodi
Kabba and his fellow Marabouts drove out many of the
older ruling classes in Kombo, Foni, Kiang, and Jarra.
Fodi Kabba and his followers came into conflict with the
British once again in 1864 with his attack upon the chief
of Yundum. The British sent a relief column to support
that traditional ruler and the Marabouts were forced to
sign another treaty of peace in 1864. Sometime after
this, Fodi Kabba resettled his family in Fuladu. What-
ever the reason for this action, it frightened Alfa Molloh and his son, Musa, who believed that Fodi Kabba
was attempting to make inroads on their power in that
Fulbe dominated kingdom. Musa attacked the village and
killed or kidnapped the entire family of Fodi Kabba.
The family remnant was released upon the personal in-
tercession of Governor D'Arcy. However, Musa's action
ushered in a new level of violence along the south bank
which had been relatively free of the marauding so
prevalent in the north bank areas. Fodi Kabba came to
rule over three districts which were isolated from one
another. One was south of Bintang Creek, another was
in western Jarra and eastern Kiang, and the last was
in a part of eastern Jarra. In between these three territories the Soninke managed to maintain a precarious
kind of existence. Fodi Kabba did not attempt to establish a centralized state such as Ma Bâ had attempted
or that Musa Molloh would create. This failure meant
that in the 1870s, raids, looting, and burning were endemic throughout the frontier areas adjacent to Fodi
Kabba's territories. Because of the ill feeling between
Fodi Kabba and Musa Molloh, the land between Jarra
and Fuladu was particularly hard hit. The division of
the Senegambia between France and Britain in 1889
brought considerable pressure to bear upon Fodi Kabba.
He was viewed by the British as one of the primary
disturbers of the peace and one of the reasons why the
slave trade continued along the southern banks of the
Gambia River. His adherents and those of Fodi Silla
threatened the members of the International Boundary
Commission. After this, Fodi Kabba retired to a station in the Casamance, but returned in the following

year to raid the Wolof in Foni. The British in January
1892 attacked him, destroyed one of his main stockaded
towns, and forced him to retire again into French territory. From his new base in the Casamance, he continued to support those Gambians who were discontented
with the new British rule. His adherents would enter
British territory, raid villages, take prisoners, and
then recross the border into French territory before any
effective pursuit could be organized. Such raids continued for almost ten years until the murder of Travelling Commissioners Sitwell and Silva at Sankandi in
1900. This town was known to be allied to Fodi Kabba
and the British Colonial authorities decided to destroy
his power once and for all. Shortages of troops due to
the South African War postponed the punitive expedition
until 1901. The British were joined by the French, and
in a two-pronged attack directed against Fodi Kabba,
Sankandi was taken and Fodi Kabba's territory on the
British side was pacified very quickly. The second
phase of the campaign was carried out directly against
the main Marabout force, and in March 1901, his fortified town of Medina was taken and Fodi Kabba was
killed. This action brought to an end a 50-year career
which spanned the entirety of the Soninke-Marabout
Wars in the Senegambia.

KABILO-TIYO. In Mandingo kingdoms, the kabilo-tiyo was
in charge of a kabilo or a collection of yards. He was
normally the senior man of a particular lineage.

KAH, KEBBA A. H. Teacher and politician born to an Islamic Wolof family at Medina Mas Kah in the Protectorate in 1934. He was educated in Koranic schools,
the Catholic mission school, and the Teachers Training
College. Kah taught at a number of Protectorate
schools until he resigned to enter politics in 1959. He
was at first affiliated with the United Party and was
elected to the Assembly in 1960. When. P. S. N'Jie
became Chief Minister, Kah was appointed to head the
Ministry of Health. After the 1962 election, he changed
his affiliation to the People's Progressive Party and was
appointed to head the Ministry of Finance and later that
of Works and Communication before being chosen to
serve as Minister of Health in 1965.

KANTORA. The uppermost of the Mandingo controlled kingdoms lying on the south bank of the Gambia River. The

rulers and traders of Kantora are mentioned in 15th-century Portuguese accounts because of their alleged possession of great quantities of gold. Kantora was one of the Mandingo states which the Molloh's attempted to absorb into Fuladu during the Soninke-Marabout conflicts in the 1870s. Although they were never completely successful, the older traditional rule in Kantora was broken. In the British reorganization of the chiefdoms of the Gambia in the 20th century, the area of the ancient kingdom and its name was revived as a District in the Upper River Division.

KEMINTANG. A Soninke chief who in the 1820s was contesting with Kolli, the chief of Kataba, for the overlordship of Niani. The power relationships were partially upset by Kolli's ceding the Island of Lemain (MacCarthy Island) to the British in 1823. But the British could not maintain a force large enough on the island to bring peace to the adjoining areas, and the endemic warfare continued. In 1834, a dispute arose between Kemintang and a Bathurst merchant at Tendeba, and Kemintang seized a vessel belonging to another merchant and held it for ransom until the British would redress the wrongs he had suffered. Instead, Lieutenant-Governor Rendall declared an embargo on upper river trade and in August despatched a 120-man force against the chief. Kemintange retired to Dungaseen, a fortified town near the headwaters of Sami Creek. The invaders dragged their cannon and ammunition through 20 miles of sand and mud only to find the walls of the town impervious to artillery. Abandoning the guns, two of which could still be used, they retreated to the Gambia River. Kemintang mounted these guns on the walls of his town, and his victory gave him added prestige in Niumi. Despite a number of British efforts, he refused to surrender the artillery, and continued to make sporadic war against Kataba until his death in 1843.

KENNEDY, SIR ARTHUR. Appointed Governor of the Gambia in 1851, but never took up the post. Between 1852 and 1854, he administered the Colony of Sierra Leone, and in 1868 he was appointed Governor of the West African Settlements and became one of the key figures in the negotiations for the exchange of British possessions in the Gambia for French territory elsewhere. The Colonial Office, responding to French offers, ordered

Kennedy to investigate and report on the situation in
the Gambia. In 1869, he visited Bathurst for the first
time and spent 10 days in the Gambia. Thus the detailed reports on conditions in the territory submitted
to the Colonial Office during the following six years
were not based on personal observation or detailed
knowledge, but on reports from subordinates and merchants who did have experience of Gambian conditions.
Despite this obvious lack of firsthand knowledge, the
Colonial Office viewed Kennedy as their expert. Even
before his visit to Bathurst, Kennedy was in favor of
some exchange that would consolidate West African territories claimed by both nations. Kennedy further
argued that the Gambia was a useless appendage which
cost Britain in military expenditures more than the
territory was worth. What trade there was, was in the
hands of French merchants, and the "peculiar population" was resistant to all attempts to extend civilization
to the areas outside the Colony. Kennedy's first long
reports along with similar ones from the administrator,
Rear Admiral Patey, convinced the British government
to propose to France a sweeping exchange of territory.
By March 1870, all the details of the exchange had
been worked out except the rights of English and French
subjects in the ceded territories. However, the Franco-
Prussian War interrupted the negotiations for exchange
and discussions were not resumed until 1875. Kennedy
left West Africa in 1872.

KESSELLIKUNDA. A town in Fuladu which was the residence
of Musa Molloh after his movement in 1903 from the
Casamance into British territory. The British recognized Musa Molloh's position as head of British Fuladu
and paid him a handsome stipend until they could no
longer ignore his practice of slavery and rumored
atrocities. In 1919, they pulled down his compound at
Kessillikunda and exiled Musa to Sierra Leone.

KIANG. One of the nine Mandingo kingdoms located along the
south bank of the Gambia River in the early 19th century. It stretched from the juncture of Bintang Bolon
and the Gambia River eastward to a point opposite
Devils Point. Bintang Bolon separated Kiang from Foni
on the south. The major port towns of Tankular and
Tendeba are in Kiang. Because of its location and
wealth, Kiang was a major prize in the Soninke-Marabout conflicts. Ma Bâ's attempt to gain a firm foothold

on the south bank was thwarted at Quinella in Kiang.
Eastern Kiang by the 1870s was firmly controlled by
Fodi Kabba while the central and western parts were
still in the hands of the Soninke or owed allegiance to
Fodi Silla. Kiang continued to be an area of disorder
until after the killing of Travelling Commissioners Sitwell and Silva and a large part of their force at Sankandi in 1900. After the British reorganization of the
Protectorate in the 20th century, Kiang was placed in
the Central Division and divided into three Districts,
each under the direction of a chief.

KILHAM, HANNAH. A member of the Society of Friends
who in 1823 arrived in the Gambia as the leader of
one of the first industrial missionary endeavors sent
to Africa. The two European men of this group
started an agricultural school at Cape St. Mary while
Mrs. Kilham and another woman, Anne Thompson,
opened a school for girls in Bathurst. Later a Wesleyan missionary arrived in the Gambia and Mrs. Kilham turned her school over to them and took up residence in Bakau where she opened another girls' school.
Within a few months all the members of the Friend's
mission were stricken with fever and were forced to
return to England, thus ending the Quaker experiment
in Westernized technical education.

KING'S BOYS. Recaptive slaves who had served with the
Royal African Corps and the West Indian Regiments
and had been pensioned or discharged. They were the
first of the Liberated Africans to be sent to the Gambia. Beginning in the early 1820s, a number of these
ex-soldiers settled along Oyster Creek with grants of
land and free farming implements. Some of the King's
Boys became government ferrymen, others burned lime
from the oyster shells for the Bathurst market, and
still others found employment in the construction of the
first public buildings in Bathurst.

KOMBO. One of the traditional south bank Mandingo kingdoms. The rulers of Kombo controlled the lands adjacent to the mouth of the Gambia River. The peoples
of Kombo had long been in contact with Europeans because of its location. Captain Grant purchased St.
Mary's Island on which to build the town of Bathurst
(Banjul) from the king of Kombo. The price was an
annual payment of 103 iron bars (approximately £25).

Later in 1853, the British negotiated a further cession
of land from Suling Jatta, another ruler of Kombo.
This new area became British Kombo, and the trans-
action helped to precipitate the Soninke-Marabout conflict in the lower river territories. The wars began
in the Kombo with the activities of Omar of Sabaji and
Fodi Kabba. The greatest threat to the continued
British presence on the river came from the warfare
between the contending factions in Kombo in the mid-
1850s. The problem was not resolved until 1855 when
Suling Jatta was killed and the Marabouts loyal to Fodi
Kabba controlled western Kombo.

KONKO. A short handled adze-shaped tool which is used for
planting peanuts. The sower uses the konko in one hand
to make holes in the ground while with the other hand
he drops the seeds into the holes.

KORDU-TIYO. The Protectorate Ordinance of 1902 and all
those which followed until 1933 accepted the yard as
the basic political institution throughout the Gambia.
A yard was defined as a collection of several huts
which had at one time been held by a kindred grouping.
The head of a yard was normally referred to by the
Mandingo term kordu-tiyo. These local leaders were
each under the supervision of the village head called
the satiyo-tiyo.

KORTRIGHT, SIR CORNELIUS H. Administrator of the Gambia from 1873 to 1875 who was deeply involved in the
1874-76 Colonial Office plans to cede the Gambia to
France. He acted as the chief source for the Colonial
Office planners. His report that Bathurst mercantile
opinion would not be hostile if proper compensation was
paid proved to be wrong since opposition from this section became very organized and vocal. Kortright was
promoted to Governor of the British West African Settlements (Sierra Leone and the Gambia) in 1875 and
held this post for two years.

KOTO, MANSA. The chief of Battelling whose town was
selected by Travelling Commissioner F. C. Sitwell in
1900 as the neutral ground to adjudicate the quarrel
between Marabouts and Soninkes in Kiang. When Dari
Bana Dabo, the Marabout leader of Sankandi, refused
to parley, Mansa Koto and some of his retainers accompanied Sitwell and his party to Sankandi. When the

people of Sankandi opened fire, Mansa Koto was killed
along with the Travelling Commissioner and the bulk of
the armed escort.


-L-

LAHAMIN JAY.  A Mandingo-speaking Fulbe who had been
    captured, sold into slavery, and sent to Maryland with
    Job ben Soloman.  Job, after his release, petitioned
    the Duke of Montagu to secure the release of Lahamin
    Jay who was returned to the Gambia by the Royal Afri-
    can Company in 1738.  He became a part of the mis-
    sion headed by Melchoir de Jaspas in 1740 which sought
    to improve trade between the company and the kingdom
    of Bondu.

LAIDLEY, DR. JOHN.  A surgeon who in 1791 joined Robert
    Aynsley, a trader, at his station at Pisania (Karantaba).
    He acted as the banker for Major Daniel Houghton and
    later Mungo Park in their expeditions into the western
    Sudan.  Park spent the latter six months of 1795 at
    Laidley's house while studying Mandingo, and it was to
    Laidley's house that he returned after his successful
    exploration.

LAMINE, MOMADU.  A Muslim leader from Bondu who had
    contested French domination and was driven to take
    refuge at Toubacouta where he was welcomed by the
    son of Simotto Moro.  A French expedition followed
    Lamine to the Gambia, and Musa Molloh, then an ally
    of the French, crossed the Gambia River with a large
    army.  The combined forces took Toubacouta in 1886
    and Momadu Lamine, according to legend, was killed
    by Musa.

LEGISLATIVE COUNCIL.  One of two councils utilized in
    British colonies to assist the governor in making de-
    cisions.  The small nominated Gambian Legislative
    Council was first created in 1843.  When the Gambia
    was made dependent on Sierra Leone in 1866, its coun-
    cil was abolished only to be reestablished after the Gam-
    bia was constituted a separate colony in 1888.  In 1893,
    the authority of the Council to make rules and orders
    was extended to the Protectorate.  In 1915, the Council
    was enlarged to include four official and three nominated
    unofficial members.  In 1932, its size was increased by

an additional African member nominated by the Urban
District Council and by one of the Commissioners from
the Protectorate. The Council was reorganized in 1947
to contain three ex-officio members, three nominated
government officials, six unofficial nominated members,
and one elected member from Bathurst. In 1951 the
number of elected members was increased to two. By
the constitutional revision of 1954, there were five ex-
officio official members, two nominated officials, seven
directly elected members from the Colony, and seven
indirectly elected from the Protectorate. After 1954,
certain elected members were appointed to the Executive Council and allowed a share in directing the affairs
of the government departments. Although they were not
yet really responsible, this was the necessary first step
toward ministerial government. According to the Constitution of 1960, the legislative instrument for the Gambia was renamed the House of Representatives.

LEMAIN ISLAND. An important trading site for trans-Gambian trade from areas in Senegal to the north as well
as from the upper Casamance. Europeans had maintained temporary trading stations on the island since
Jobson's time. In 1823, the British gained possession
of Lemain Island and renamed it MacCarthy Island in
honor of the governor-in-chief of the British West African Territories.

LIBERATED AFRICANS. Africans in transit as slaves to the
new world who were liberated, normally by warships of
the British West African Patrol. Because they were
taken twice, the term Recaptive came to be used to
describe these Africans. Most of the recaptives were
taken to Freetown, although they came from various
parts of West Africa and represented many different
tribes and cultural groups. They presented a considerable problem to the British government in Freetown
which had only limited funds available for resettlement.
Many of the recaptives in the 1820s and 1830s found
their way to the Gambia where they became the nucleus
of a Westernized population in Bathurst. The Akus
(Yoruba) became particularly important in trade and
commerce, and their descendants were among the first
to occupy important posts in the civil service and government of 20th-century Gambia.

LLEWELLYN, SIR RICHARD B. Administrator of the Gambia,

1891-1901.  He was the man most responsible for establishing the early forms of Indirect Rule in the Protectorate.  British control over most of the Gambia
River areas after the Convention of 1889 had been exercised in an ad hoc intermittent manner until 1893 when
Llewellyn appointed the first Travelling Commissioner.
After months of study of other British Colonial dependencies, particularly India, the governor and his staff
issued the Protectorate Ordinance of 1894.  Later
governors modified this legislation, but the basic form
and mechanics of Protectorate government as stated in
the 1894 Ordinance remained in effect until the eve of
Gambian independence.  Llewellyn was also primarily
responsible for modifying the more extreme demands
of the French representatives on the various boundary
commissions of the 1890s.  He and his advisors drew
up and instituted the plans for the joint operation with
the French in 1901 which finally destroyed the influence
of Fodi Kabba.


                                -M-


MCP   see  MUSLIM CONGRESS PARTY

MacCARTHY, SIR CHARLES.  Governor-in-Chief of the
    British West African Territories (1814-1824) who made
    the recommendation to the Colonial Office in 1815 that
    Britain reoccupy James Island.  He supported Captain
    Alexander Grant in his decision not to attempt the re-
    building of the fort on the island, but rather to purchase
    Banjul (St. Mary's) Island from the king of Kombo and
    build the British base there.  Although until 1821 the
    government of the Gambia was military and seemingly
    of a temporary nature, MacCarthy had enlisted the sup-
    port of the newly arrived Bathurst merchants for the
    government, and he had established a courts system.
    After 1821, the Gambia was officially made a part of
    the British West African Territories he controlled from
    his headquarters in Freetown.  In 1824, MacCarthy was
    killed at Bonsaso in the Gold Coast while leading his
    troops in an abortive invasion of Ashantiland.  Mac-
    Carthy Island was subsequently named for him.

MacCARTHY ISLAND.  Called Lemain Island in the 18th
    century, it was the site of temporary trading stations
    from the time of Jobson.  In 1823, the British took

possession of the island and despite much pressure
from the Soninke-Marabout Wars and a penurious treasury, it remained throughout the century their chief
enclave in the interior.  Georgetown, one of the larger
towns of the interior, is located on the island.

MacDONNELL, SIR RICHARD GRAVES.  Governor of the
    Gambia from 1847 until early 1852.  In 1844 while
    serving as first Chief Justice of the Colony, he made
    one of the longest journeys into the hinterland seeking
    information on the people, their customs, and potential
    trade.  He travelled by water to Fattatenda where he
    met three Frenchmen who had just visited Bondu.
    From Fattatenda he travelled on foot to the capital of
    Bondu where he induced the ruler to repudiate the ex-
    clusive trade treaty he had just made with the French-
    men, and extracted a promise that the route from
    Bondu to the Gambia River would be kept open.  After
    being appointed governor, MacDonnell in 1849 and 1850
    undertook yet other explorations.  In 1849 he travelled
    by boat over 100 miles beyond Barrakunda Falls.  In
    the following year he reached Jallakotta on the Neriko
    River.  He was disappointed by both expeditions since
    he found the river above the falls difficult to navigate,
    the country sparsely settled, and little sign of major
    cultivation of any exportable crop.  On the return jour-
    ney in 1850, Governor MacDonnell's party narrowly es-
    caped death when he visited Kunnong near Quinella.  The
    inhabitants of Kunnong, after driving off MacDonnell,
    then pillaged a trading post nearby.  On his return to
    Bathurst, MacDonnell organized a punitive expedition
    which eventually forced the chief of Kunnong to signify
    his submission to the British governor.  Earlier in
    1849, MacDonnell had helped organize a joint French-
    British expedition against the Papels on Bissago
    Island who had made a practice of capturing shipwrecked
    vessels and their crews.

MacNAMARA, MATTHIAS.  An Ensign in O'Hara's Corps in
    the Senegambia who was selected over senior officers
    to be Lieutenant-Governor at James Island in 1774.
    He disobeyed orders, seized French trading ships, and
    traded privately with the Africans.  Despite such ac-
    tions, he became the Governor of Senegambia in late
    1775.  Almost immediately he began a quarrel with
    Captain Wall who had taken his place at James Island.
    MacNamara ordered Wall's arrest and kept him in

confinement for 10 months at the fort before bringing
him to trial. Wall was subsequently cleared of the
charges and in two civil suits won damages from Mac-
Namara who was removed as Governor of Senegambia
by the Council of Trade in August 1778.

MAHONEY, SIR JOHN. One of the leaders of the Bathurst
community in the second quarter of the 20th century.
He was the recognized leader of the Mahoney family
which counted some of the most educated and influential
people in Bathurst. Some of these were the lawyer
Jacob Mahoney, the eventual Minister of Health, John
Mahoney and his wife, Florence, the first Gambian
Ph.D., and Augusta, the first wife of Prime Minister
Jawara. Sir John was a longtime friend of Edward
Small and other early nationalists, and in the 1940s
was a nominated member of the Legislative Council.
In the early 1950s, he became the Speaker of the Legislative Council, and just before his retirement, he was
named the Speaker of the House of Representatives in
1960.

MALI EMPIRE. After the Almoravids overthrew the kingdom
of Ghana in the 11th century, there ensued a century
and a half of military and commercial rivalry between
a number of powerful city states of the western Sudan.
Eventually in the 13th century, the Mandingo ruler
Sundiata defeated his Soso rivals. On the base of Sundiata's conquests, later rulers built the Malian empire,
the most powerful and richest empire ever developed
in the Sudan. It reached its apex under Mansa Musa
in the 14th century, its fame being underscored by
Mansa Musa's legendary trip to Mecca. Before its
downfall, the empire included eastern Senegal, and
many Gambian riverine rulers paid homage and tribute
to the great king of Mali.

MALTA PLAN. In the late 1950s, this was one solution suggested for small British dependencies which were considered to be too weak or economically nonviable to become totally independent. It was at first proposed to
solve the problem of the island of Malta, and was also
proposed for the Gambia. The chief feature of the plan
was some type of federal association between the dependent territories and Great Britain. With the political
leaders of most of the smaller areas opting for independence, the plan was abandoned even before details of
association were seriously discussed.

MANDINGO.  One of the most important people resident in
     the Gambia.  In present-day Gambia, they comprise
     over 40 per cent of the estimated population.  The Man-
     dingo are spread fairly evenly throughout the length of
     the country.  The Gambian Mandingo are the most
     westerly extension of the Manding group of people who
     speak kindred languages of the northern sub-group of
     the Niger-Congo family of languages and have similar
     political and social organizations.  Some of the other
     West African Manding speakers are the Bambara, Dyula,
     and Kuranko.  The Mandingo people are long resident
     in the Gambia, probably moving into the area during the
     period of disorder in the western Sudan following the
     breakup of the empire of Ghana in the 11th century.
     Richard Jobson noted in the 17th century that Mandingo
     rulers in the Gambia still showed deference to the ruler
     of Mali long after the breakdown of its hegemony over
     the western Sudan.  Mandingo society was divided into
     three endogamous castes--the freeborn (foro), slaves
     (jongo), and artisans or praise singers (nyamalo).  Age
     groups (kafo) were important in Mandingo society in
     contrast to the socio-political organizations of neighbor-
     ing Wolof people.  The basis of life for the Mandingo
     was and is agriculture, although they were also the
     dominant traders on the river.  In the latter 19th cen-
     tury, cultivation of peanuts became the major concern
     for most Mandingo farmers.
          In the 19th century almost all the riverine terri-
     tories of the Gambia were controlled by a number of
     Mandingo rulers (mansa) through the medium of related
     but separate and competing kingdoms.  These were
     Niumi, Jokadu, Baddibu, Upper and Lower Niani, and
     Wuli on the north bank, and Kombo, Foni, Kiang, Jarra,
     Niamina, Eropina, Jimara, Tomani, and Kantora along
     the south bank.  Rule in each of these states was based
     upon kinship and each king surrounded himself with his
     own complex bureaucracy.  The kingdoms were sub-
     divided into territorial units of the village, ward, and
     family compound.  Village administration was carried
     out by the satiyo-tiyo (alkali) in council.  Each village
     was further divided into kabilos or wards which were
     administered by a kabilo-tiyo.  Each of these officials
     was chosen on a basis of his lineage as well as
     his abilities.  The kings each maintained an armed
     force to defend the state and impose their will on their
     subjects.  Since they were not permitted to lead troops,
     the rulers chose a general (jawara) for this function.

The Mandingo systems of rule were challenged in the latter 19th century by proselytizing teachers who wished to convert the Mandingo to Islam.  The conflicts which ensued led to the half century series of wars called the Soninke-Marabout Wars which resulted in the conversion of most of the people to Islam and a breakdown of traditional Mandingo authority structures in the Gambia.

MANE, KOLLI MANKE.  King of Barra at the time when Alexander Grant began the construction of the first buildings in Bathurst.  The king allowed the British to quarry stone on Dog Island and made no stipulation for direct payment.  Undoubtedly this was done because Grant in 1816 reordered the method of payment whereby the king benefitted more directly from customs duties than previously.  Nevertheless, after Kollimanke Mane's death in 1823, this incident was remembered by the new king and his advisors, and was one of the latent reasons for the Barra War of 1831.

MANSA.  Mandingo title for the king of one of their traditional states.

MARABOUTS.  Initially Muslim religious teachers who later came to exercise considerable political and economic influence.  At the court of every Senegambian ruler who had accepted Islam, there would be at least one Marabout whose responsibilities in normal times were to pray for the ruler, give advice, and handle correspondence.  In the disturbed conditions after 1850, some of the Marabouts came to wield great political influence, and some such as Ma Bâ became themselves the rulers of large kingdoms.  This was the case in many areas adjacent to the Gambia River where traditional rulers and their entourages refused to accept Islam.  The series of civil wars called the Soninke-Marabout Wars were initially based on the desires of reforming Marabouts to overthrow the "pagan" traditional rulers and convert the people to Islam.

M'BAKI, OMAR.  Politician and former seyfu of Sami District.  One of the few educated chiefs in the Gambia in the late 1950s.  He served for 14 years as a member of the Executive Council during British rule.  After the election of 1960, he was a minister in the government of P. S. N'Jie and was the spokesman for the indirectly elected Protectorate chiefs.  At this time he was considered

by some as a political alternative to the leaders of the
two major parties.   When the People's Progressive
Party came to power, he managed a compromise with
Sir Dauda Jawara and the other government leaders.
However, in 1965 he and six other chiefs were dismissed by the central government for anti-government
attitudes.

MEDICAL RESEARCH COUNCIL.   One of the major African
tropical research units established at Fajara soon after
World War II and maintained by the Medical Research
Council of Great Britain and by Colonial Development
funds.   Later a field station was established at Keneba.
A 40-bed research ward was maintained at Fajara.   The
staff comprised a director, six medical and scientific
officers, a number of expatriate staff, and over 75
Gambians.   The establishment was engaged in the study
of tropical diseases, particularly malaria, sickle cell
anemia, and filariasis.   The facilities were regularly
made available to qualified visitors to carry out their
own researches.

MOLLOH, ALFA (Molloh Egue).   The creator of the state of
Fuladu and one of the main participants in the Soninke-
Marabout Wars in the upper river during the 1870s.   A
member of the Fulbe Firdu, he was born Molloh Egue
in the old Mandingo kingdom of Jimara, probably in the
third decade of the 19th century.   He was an elephant
hunter, and had gained a great reputation with arms
before a disagreement with the ruler of Jimara caused
him to lead a revolt of the Fulbe against the traditional
rulers.   It was rumored that he had met with Al Hajj
Umar and had taken the Tijaniyya oath before 1867.
His devotion to Islam, however, appears to have been
more a matter of expediency than true devotion.   It did
gain him support from the Islamic states of the Futa
Jallon and Futa Toro.   His forces in a five-year period
conquered Jimara, Tomani, and a number of smaller
chieftancies southward to the Casamance, and then laid
the foundations for the centralized state of Fuladu, constructed largely with the conquests of his son Musa.
Molloh Egue, soon after his initial conquest, assumed
the name of Alfa Molloh.   Alfa did not hesitate to use
armed forces to subdue potential rivals, and his chief
agent in establishing control over the Fulbe was Musa
and his army.   After Alfa's death in 1881, Fuladu was
torn by internecine strife because according to the

matrilineal succession, Alfa's brother, Bakari Dembel, inherited the throne.

MOLLOH, MUSA. The son of Alfa Molloh, founder of the
Fulbe kingdom of Fuladu. During the decade of the
1870s, Musa was content to act as the commander of
his father's military forces, and it was he more than
any other person who expanded the areas under the
control of Alfa at the expense of the traditional Mandingo rulers as well as those of such other Marabouts
as Fodi Kabba and Simotto Moro. The death of Alfa
Molloh in 1881 fractured the recently created state of
Fuladu since Musa had no intention of meekly surrendering his power to his uncle who had inherited the
throne. Musa took his faction southward, established
a fortified base at Hamdallai, and in 1883 placed himself under the protection of the French. With their
aid he soon reestablished his authority throughout much
of Fuladu, and eventually killed his uncle and other
members of the family who stood in his way of maintaining control of the state. Finally in 1892, he proclaimed himself king. The state which Musa Molloh
created was a reflection of his need for a stable kingdom which would respond quickly to his desires. He
exercised complete military authority and controlled the
political life of the state by a close watch over the 40
district leaders he appointed to act in his name throughout the territory. Musa also used a central bureaucracy
to check on the activities of the district heads. Unfortunately for Musa's centralized state, the partition
of the Senegambia after 1889 brought fundamental changes
to Fuladu. It was clear to Musa that in order to maintain the unity of his kingdom, he would have to choose
peace rather than war with the Europeans, and he therefore promised to live quietly in the newly established
French territory. In 1901, he participated in the joint
expedition against his old enemy, Fodi Kabba. However, with the arrival of more French and British authorities in the interior, the days of his freedom of
action were almost at an end. The French interfered
more and more with his rule, particularly as the rumors
of his tyranny against his subjects reached the centers
of authority. In 1903, the French decided to build a
military post at Hamdallai. In response, Musa burned
his town, cut the telegraph lines, and retreated to
British territory where he established himself at Kessellikunda. The British recognized his control over what

was then only a small portion of his once large kingdom. They paid him an annual stipend and in general
left his rule alone. Without an army and cut off from
the bulk of his previous territory in the south, he was
actually a British prisoner. They could depose him
whenever they wished. It was merely to their advantage to have such a strong ruler who acted as a unifying force in the upriver areas. In 1919, finally
reacting to reports of atrocities, the British deposed
Musa, pulled down his royal compound, and exiled him
to Sierra Leone. He was allowed to return in 1923,
shorn almost entirely of his power. Until his death in
1931, he remained nothing but a shadowy reminder of
the time when he was the most powerful of the kings
of the southern Senegambia.

MOLONEY, CAPTAIN C. ALFRED. Administrator of the
Gambia from 1884 to 1885. His major contribution
during his brief tenure was the completion of the 300-
yard-long bridge over Oyster Creek.

MOORE, FRANCIS. Representative of the Royal African
Company and writer, who was sent to James Island in
1730. During his nearly five years stay in the Gambia, Moore travelled throughout much of the area. He
was a trade factor in many places, most notably at
Joar and Yamyamacunda. Much of our knowledge of
Gambian social, economic, and political institutions in
the 18th century is due to Moore's keen interest in the
riverine Africans and their customs. His observations
were published in 1735 in what became one of the classic books detailing West African life, Travels in the
Inland Parts of Africa.

MUMBO JUMBO. Described by Francis Moore in the 18th
century as a figure of considerable importance in Mandingo society. He was a man dressed in leaves who
was called upon to judge the virtue of persons in a
particular village. He spoke a particular secret cant
language not understandable to women or outsiders.
(The origin of the English usage of the term.)

MUSLIM CONGRESS PARTY (MCP). The second political
party in the Gambia, it was formed from the Bathurst
Young Muslim Society and a number of smaller asso-
ciations by I. M. Garba-Jahumpa in January 1952. It
sought to join religious affiliation with political activity.

In this, the party was not successful, although individual members did gain some political standing.  Garba-Ja-humpa in the 1950s continued to work closely with the Colonial government as a member of the Bathurst Town Council and as one of the elected members of the Legislative Council.  In retrospect, this cooperation damaged the image of the Muslim Congress Party, and it became apparent before the elections of 1960 that the United Party was likely to sweep the elected seats in Bathurst.  In order to obtain a broader support base, the leaders of the Muslim Congress Party agreed in 1960 to merge their party with the Democratic Party to form a new grouping called the Democratic Congress Alliance.  After the failure of the DCA to become a major factor in Gambian politics, Garba-Jahumpa led his supporters into creating a new Congress Party.  By 1968, Garba-Jahumpa had settled his major differences with the ruling People's Progressive Party, and the Congress Party was disbanded.


-N-


NENYO.   The caste to which the Wolof assigned artisans and various technicians.   Smiths, leatherworkers, wood-workers, and the gewels or praise singers belonged to this caste.

NIAMINA.   One of the nine Mandingo-controlled kingdoms located along the south bank of the Gambia River in the early 19th century, located directly east and south of the river as it makes the great bend to the east.   By the late 1870s, most of the traditional rulers had been driven out or had assumed a subordinate position to Fodi Kabba.   Niamina was the most westerly extension of the kingdom of Fuladu, and therefore the eastern section was a battleground between the Marabout forces and those of the Mollohs'.   During the 20th-century British reorganization of the Protectorate, Niamina was joined with the territory of the old Mandingo kingdom of Eropina.   This composite was placed in the Mac-Carthy Island Division, then sub-divided into three Dis-tricts, each under the direction of a chief.

NIANI.   A north bank area which stretches from Nianiji Bolon on the west to Sandugu Bolon on the east.   In the early 19th century, this large territory was divided into two

Mandingo-dominated kingdoms. In the 1830s, Kemintang
caused considerable disturbance in the area and for a
time dominated Upper Niani despite British attempts to
defeat him. The ruler of Lower Niani whose base was
at Kataba maintained excellent relations with the British
in the 1840s, dating from the time when British military forces protected him from Kemintang. Despite the
practice of allowing Marabouts a premier place in the
kingdoms, Niani became a major battleground in the
Soninke-Marabout Wars. Bounded on the west by Ma
Bâ's kingdom of Baddibu (Rip) and on the east by Wuli,
which was dominated by Bakari Sardu, the territory was
ravaged by a series of competing armies. Later in the
1880s, the contending forces of Mamadou N'Dare and
Saër Maty continued the unrest in Niani. Niani was
divided into two Districts in the 20th-century British
reorganization of the Protectorate. Upper Niani was
renamed Sami. Each District was placed under the
direction of a chief.

NIUMI. One of the five major north bank kingdoms controlled
in the early 19th century by Mandingo rulers. Niumi
was strategically located fronting on the Atlantic Ocean
and dominating the entrance to the Gambia River. Because of its physical locale, Niumi was early in contact with the Europeans. In 1826, the British negotiated
a treaty whereby the entire river frontage of Niumi
passed to the British as the Ceded Mile. They proceeded immediately to build Fort Bullen which would
help command the entrance into the Gambia River. Difficulties over this cession caused the Barra War of
1830-31. During the Soninke-Marabout Wars, Niumi
was a major battleground, as first Ma Bâ and then his
lieutenants sought to add the territory to the kingdom of
Rip (Baddibu). Amer Faal was the most important of
the Marabouts in Niumi who from his base at Tubab
Kolon continued to raid through the area until a combined British and Soninke force took his fortified town
in 1866. Thereafter there was relative peace in Niumi
largely because the British considered the security of
Niumi vital for the maintenance of their authority in the
Ceded Mile. In the 20th-century reorganization of the
Protectorate, the area became a District in the Lower
River Division and the ruler of Niumi was considered
one of the most important chiefs of the Protectorate.

N'JIE, ALHAJI A. B. Civil servant and politician, born of

a Wolof family in Bathurst in 1904. Although their
names are the same, he is not related to Pierre or
Ebrimah N'Jie. He attended Methodist mission schools
in Bathurst and entered the Civil Service in 1925. He
held a number of positions and retired in 1958 as the
Registrar of the Supreme Court. Although a Muslim,
he opposed the concept held by the Muslim Congress of
using religion for political purposes, and instead helped
form the Democratic Party. He headed a number of
ministries before being appointed in the late 1960s as
Minister of State for External Affairs and Resident
Minister in Dakar. In the reshuffle of the ministry
after Gambia became a Republic, he was made Minister
of Information, and in 1971 was appointed Minister of
State at the President's Office.

N'JIE, EBRIMAH DOWDA. Lawyer, civil servant, and poli-
    tician, and one of the founder members of the United
    Party. Unlike his brother, Pierre Sarr N'Jie, Ebrimah
    tended to stay in the background. Although a member
    of the House of Representatives and a minister in his
    brother's government of 1961, he did not aspire to high
    office. He was a competent lawyer who devoted much
    of his time to the law firm which he shared with his
    brothers. A rift in the United Party in May 1970
    caused the party to depose P. S. N'Jie as leader and
    elect Ebrimah to succeed him. However, before his
    leadership could really be tested, he was killed in an
    automobile accident in 1972.

N'JIE, PIERRE SARR. A Bathurst barrister and politician,
    born July 17, 1909, and educated at St. Augustine's
    School. While in his early 20s, he worked in a series
    of government departments including the Public Works
    Department. He eventually became an assistant Clerk
    of the Courts. In 1943, he left for England and served
    briefly in the Royal Artillery. He began his legal
    training in 1944 at Lincoln's Inn and was called to the
    bar in 1948. He returned to the Gambia and began
    practicing law in Bathurst. In 1951, he was defeated
    for an elected seat on the Legislative Council. Shortly
    afterward, he and other Wolof formed the United Party.
    In 1954, he was elected to the Legislative Council at
    the head of the poll. The following year he disagreed
    openly with Governor Wyn Harris and resigned from the
    government. His absence from government proved for-
    tunate since he escaped the stigma of appearing to be

controlled by the British.  In the elections of 1960 for
an expanded House of Representatives, the United Party
returned six members, although the newly formed People's Progressive Party showed great popular strength
in the Protectorate.  In 1961, because of his rapport
with the Protectorate chiefs, N'Jie was appointed Chief
Minister.  However, in the 1962 elections, the United
Party could gain only 13 seats to the PPP's 18 and
P. S. N'Jie became the leader of the opposition.  The
influence of the United Party continued to decline after
Gambian independence despite its power base in the old
Colony area and its coalitions with other Gambian parties.  N'Jie's popularity also waned, and in May 1970,
he was replaced as leader of the United Party by his
brother, E. D. N'Jie.  After his brother's death in
1972, the party once more elected P. S. as leader.
In 1973, his political fortunes reached a nadir when he
was removed from the roster of the House of Representatives because of non-attendance.

NOHOR.  Wolof term which distinguishes a person whose
father was <u>dema</u> but whose mother was not a witch.
They are believed to be gifted with second sight, but
cannot otherwise do harm.

NYAMALO.  The title given in Mandingo society to the low
born caste of artisans or praise singers, comparable
to the Wolof <u>nenyo</u>.


-O-


O'CONNOR, LUKE S. (COLONEL).  Governor of the Gambia
from 1852 to 1859 and Commander in Chief of British
military forces in West Africa.  He recommended a
forward policy to the home government in order to
secure Bathurst and the Colony area from the threat
of either the Marabouts or Soninke in adjacent areas.
His suggestions were not accepted, and he was forced
to follow a defensive posture in regard to those leaders
who threatened British hegemony.  He negotiated the
cession of more territory from Suling Jatta of Kombo
and this helped precipitate open conflict with Omar of
Sabaji and Fodi Kabba of Gunjur.  He sent a punitive
expedition to Sabaji in 1853, but this did not end the
problem, and two years later, Omar directed a major
thrust at the Soninkes in Kombo and their British

protectors. In June 1855, O'Connor's forces were defeated and he was wounded. Only by the most strenuous
efforts, and with the support of the king of Barra and
with French reinforcements from Senegal, was he able
to resume the offensive and capture Sabaji. In April
1856, O'Connor arranged a truce between the Marabouts
and Soninke in the Kombo. O'Connor was responsible
for major additions to the town of Bathurst; he supervised the construction of a barracks and a civil hospital,
and the Albert Market dates from his tenure. After
peace returned to the Kombos, O'Connor resumed his
practice of touring the upriver areas, attempting to
secure a rapprochement with the riverine rulers in this
brief lull in the fighting between traditionalists and
Muslims.

O'HARA, CHARLES (Colonel). An officer of the Coldstream
Guards who became, in 1765, the first Governor of the
Senegambia. He was also in command of O'Hara's
Corps comprising three companies of foot soldiers
raised specifically for the defense of the territory. One
company was posted to the Gambia and was stationed at
James Fort. O'Hara devoted most of his energies to
the problems of Senegal, leaving the lieutenant-governors
in the Gambia to deal with the problems of trade, diplomacy with Gambian chiefs, and the threat of a revived
France. Unfortunately, the lieutenant-governors tended
to disobey orders, carry on private trade, and in
general act without restraint. In 1775, the problem of
governing the Senegambia was compounded by the cruel
and arbitrary actions of Lieutenant-Governor MacNamara.
Thus when O'Hara ended his 11-year tour, the Province
was in turmoil.

OMAR OF SABAJI (Sukuta). Little is known of his life before
his arrival in the Gambia except that he was a Mauritanian and had taken part in Abd-el-Kader's uprising
against the French in Algeria in 1847, where he had
acquired a modicum of military training. In the Gambia, he moved to Sabaji where in conjunction with other
Marabouts he began to organize the population disaffected
by the forced cession of their town to the British in
1853. He was also responsible for the fiction that he
had the power to turn British bullets into water. Omar
supported Fodi Kabba in his dispute with Kombo which
led directly to the storming of the latter's town and the
death of Kombo's ruler, Suling Jatta, in June 1855. This

and further disturbances at Sabaji convinced the British governor, Colonel O'Connor, to send a small military detachment to Sabaji.  This force was driven out and retreated to Jeshwang, and after O'Connor with all of his available troops marched to their relief, he decided to take his 260 men and attack Sabaji directly.  The people of Sabaji led by Omar, and reinforced from other towns, trapped O'Connor's troops.  The British had to retreat, losing one fourth of their number in killed and wounded.  If Omar had pressed his advantage, he could have bypassed O'Connor and driven to Bathurst.  With reinforcements from Barra, Kombo, and French troops from Goree, O'Connor and the West African regiments marched to Sabaji, and after fierce fighting, took the town on July 15, 1855.  Omar escaped and fled the Gambia, presumably for Senegal, and thereafter was never a factor in the Soninke-Marabout conflicts.

ORD, H. ST. GEORGE (Colonel; later Major-General). Deputized in 1864 by Parliament to investigate the position of the British West African Settlements.  Although agreeing in the main with those critics of Colonial policy who believed that these settlements were not profitable, he did not recommend their abandonment. With special reference to the Gambia and Freetown, he concluded that Britain had a moral obligation to the African people who had sought the protection of the Crown.  He agreed with Governor D'Arcy when he stated in his 1865 report that some way should be found to extend British protection to the troubled areas on the north bank of the Gambia River.  The select Committee of Parliament used Ord's report as justification for a no-expansionist doctrine which became the official British policy for two decades.

ORFEUR, CHARLES.  Chief agent of the Royal African Company beginning in 1718.  He had joined the company only a few months before as a writer.  His attempts to repair Fort James and to improve the company's trade were interrupted by the appearance in 1719 of pirates. They sacked the fort, took a number of ships as prizes, and scattered the small garrison.  In 1721, Orfeur handed over what was left of the garrison to the new governor, Colonel Thomas Whitney.  He was supplanted in command of the trading activities by two new merchant factors.  Orfeur continued in the company's service in a subordinate position until 1723 when the death of his

superiors once more placed him in charge of the company's trading activities.  He assisted Captain Stibbs
to prepare for his upriver expedition, and commanded
one of the company ships in action in 1726 against a
would-be pirate.  In mid-1727, he gave over supreme
authority to Daniel Pepper who proceeded to loot the
company of as much as he could.  Eventually in 1737,
Orfeur was given the permanent appointment of chief
agent in the Gambia, and he endeavored to increase the
company's profits despite increasing French competition
and the resumption of the wars in 1743.  He was killed
by some of the subjects of the king of Barra in 1745
while on a trade mission.

OZANNE, J. H.  Appointed as the first Travelling Commissioner for the north bank areas in 1893.  His district
began at Suara Creek and extended past Niambantang
approximately 120 miles upriver.  Like his counterpart,
F. C. Sitwell, on the south bank, he travelled the entire area on foot, stopping at each major village to
explain their new position in the scheme of Protectorate
government.  Later he passed on the newest regulations
which had been decided on in Bathurst.  He also adjudicated disagreements between villages, and sat with
the African rulers when they heard civil or criminal
cases.  Considering the long history of disorders in
his territory, Ozanne surprisingly found little hostility
or resentment.  This was due, perhaps, to the proximity
of the French who were greatly disliked by both the people and their rulers.  Before being invalided home,
Ozanne had firmly established the basis of British rule
in the northern segments of the Protectorate.

-P-

PPA   see  SISAY, SHERIF

PPP   see  PEOPLE'S PROGRESSIVE PARTY

PALMER, SIR H. RICHMOND.  Governor of the Gambia from
1930 to 1933.  He had previously been Lieutenant-Governor of Northern Nigeria and a disciple of Lord Lugard.
In 1933, he issued his Political Memoranda for the
Guidance of Commissioners... which reflected many of
the concepts of indirect rule as enunciated by Lugard
and Sir Donald Cameron.  He also issued a series of

Ordinances in 1933 designed to regularize and stan-
dardize government and court activities in the Protectorate. In the previous year he had added a second
African member to the Legislative Council and also
appointed one of the Commissioners of the Protectorate
to the Council. This was the first time the Protectorate was directly represented in the central government. In 1931, Governor Palmer also sponsored the
formation of the advisory Urban District Council to act
as a point of contact between the people of the Colony
and the government. This organization later developed
into the Bathurst Town Council. Palmer was also an
accomplished Arabic scholar and historian, and in 1931
published The Carthaginian Voyage to West Africa in
500 B.C. together with Sultan Mohammed Bello's Account of the Origin of the Fulbe.

PARK, MUNGO. Scottish explorer, born in 1773 and died
in 1805 near Bussa in Nigeria. He was sponsored by
the African Association in 1795 to investigate the many
rumors connected with the Niger River, and he spent
some time studying Mandingo at Dr. Laidley's station
at Karantaba before leaving the Gambia on his first
expedition. After many hardships, he reached Segu
and the Niger before being forced to turn back. He
returned to the Gambia in September 1798 with definite
proof of the existence of the great river, its direction
of flow, and some knowledge of the people of the
western savannah. In 1805, Park, sponsored by the
Colonial Office, set out from the Gambia on his ill-
fated second expedition. There were far too many
Europeans in the large entourage, and the journey was
begun during the rainy season. By the time Bamako
was reached, only Park and four companions were
healthy enough to continue. They constructed a raft
and floated down the Niger as far as Bussa where
legend claims they were drowned in the rapids. Park's
journal of the second expedition was later brought to the
coast by one of his followers, Issaco. Park's two expeditions were the tangible beginnings of the drive by
Europeans to open the interior of West Africa.

PATEY, C. G. (Rear Admiral). The Administrator of the
Gambia from 1866 to 1871. He was one of the key in-
formants for the Colonial and Foreign Offices in their
attempt to exchange the Gambia for suitable territory
elsewhere in Africa. He agreed with Sir Arthur Kennedy,

his immediate supervisor, that there were few good
reasons for Britain to retain the Gambia. He reported that the cost of maintaining the garrison was
high and the bulk of the groundnut trade was already
dominated by the French. The endemic warfare between Fodi Kabba and the Soninke rulers of Kombo
fostered his belief that little could be done to improve
the Africans adjacent to the Colony. Patey's attitude
was, without doubt, colored by the disasterous cholera
epidemic which struck the Colony in late April 1869.
Before the disease had run its course, over 1100 citizens of Bathurst out of a population of 4000 died.
Patey was the Administrator during the height of the
upriver violence attendent on the rise of Alfa Molloh
and the collapse of Ma Bâ's empire.

PAUL, SIR JOHN. Governor of the Gambia from 1962 to
1965 who had the distinction of being the last British
Governor on the continent of Africa. In 1947, he
joined the Colonial Service and spent the next 15 years
in Sierra Leone as a District Officer, Provincial Officer, and Secretary to the Cabinet. In the Gambia, he
immediately established good relations with the then
Chief Minister, P. S. N'Jie, and his successor, Sir
Dauda Jawara who became the first Prime Minister.
From the first, Paul recognized that his position was
transitional and he contributed much to the framing of
Gambian proposals for independence.

PEANUTS  see  GROUNDNUTS

PEOPLE'S PROGRESSIVE ALLIANCE  see  SISAY, SHERIF

PEOPLE'S PROGRESSIVE PARTY (PPP). Originally formed
by David (now Sir Dauda) Jawara, Sanjally Bojang, and
other Protectorate leaders to contest the 1960 elections.
At first it was called the Protectorate People's Party,
but the name was changed to avoid accusations of being
divisive. Nevertheless, PPP support has remained
strongest in the Protectorate with its greatest support
among the Mandingo people. In the elections of 1960,
the PPP won eight seats to the House of Representatives
to only six for the United Party. This was counter-
balanced, however, by the eight appointed chiefs, and
when the British governor decided to appoint a Chief
Minister, he selected P. S. N'Jie, the United Party
leader, instead of Jawara. At the next election in 1962

for an expanded House where the chiefs' powers had
been greatly reduced, the PPP won 18 of the con-
tested seats.  Since then the PPP has been in control
of the Gambian government, and it was the party which
negotiated independence.  Despite a brief setback on
the question of a Presidential form of government in
1965, the PPP's power has continued to grow.  In the
elections of 1966, the PPP won 24 or the 32 elected
seats to the House.  Sir Dauda Jawara (knighted in
1966) reintroduced his proposals for Presidential government, and this time the people supported it at the ref-
erendum in April 1970.  The United Party during the
same period was undergoing a series of crises, and in
the general elections of 1972, the PPP won an overwhelming victory, gaining 28 seats while the United
Party won only three (Colony-based) seats.

PETERS, LENRIE.  Poet and Medical Officer born in Bathurst in 1932.  He was educated in secondary schools in
the Gambia and later in Sierra Leone, and at Trinity
College, Cambridge.  He graduated from medical school
in 1959 and then studied surgery at Guilford.  His first
volume of poems was published by Mbara, Ibadan in
1964.  Since then he has been recognized as one of the
finest African poets.  Returning to the Gambia he continued the practice of medicine and became the Chief
Surgeon and Director of the Protectorate Hospital at
Bansang.

PHILLIPS, MILLARD.  The poultry expert from the United
States employed by Lord Trefgarne, Chairman of the
Board of the Colonial Development Corporation, to be
the field director of the Yundum egg scheme.  Phillips
had been very successful with a similar project in the
West Indies.  However, lack of knowledge of the Gambia and a disinclination to accept advice from local officials led him and his associates to project very optimistic estimates and to downgrade the very real problems in establishing the scheme.  Grain crops met only
one-quarter of the estimated production, and most of
the chickens died of fowl pest.  In February 1951, the
corporation decided to accept their losses of almost one
million pounds, and Phillips departed from the Gambia.

PORTENDIC.  A trading station in Mauritania for those merchants who dealt in gum arabic.  British theoretical
rights to trade there were surrendered by a treaty with

France in 1857 in exchange for the cession of Albreda on the north bank of the Gambia River.

PORTUGUESE TOWN. A section of Banjul (Bathurst) which lay west of the barracks and MacCarthy Square. The section immediately fronting on the Atlantic Ocean was, in the 19th century, a residential district for the merchants. Behind this more exclusive section was the area where most of the mulatto population of the town resided.

-Q-

QADIRIYYA. The chief Muslim tariq or mystical brotherhood in western Africa in the 19th century. It was the first such tariq formed to make the doctrines of Islam more intelligible to the ordinary believer, and was created by Abd al Qadir al Gilani in the 12th century.

QUIN, THOMAS F. British merchant who was described as the most substantial trader in the Gambia in the early 1860s. He had previously been in the employ of the government. Quin was one of the most vocal opponents to the two plans to exchange the Gambia for French territory. Although his fortunes in the Gambia had declined by 1875, he remained a powerful aid to the London and Manchester Chambers of Commerce in bringing pressure to bear on the government to end the negotiations with France.

QUINELLA (Kwinella). A village in Kiang. In 1863, a son of the former Soninke ruler of Baddibu attempted to overthrow Ma Bâ's powers, and having failed, recrossed the Gambia River where he and his followers regrouped themselves near Quinella. Ma Bâ's forces pursued them across the river, and there ensued one of the major pitched battles of the Soninke-Marabout Wars. Ma Bâ was defeated, his army retreated, and he was forced briefly to seek sanctuary from the Fulbe at Sumbundu. Although this defeat was not as important a factor in the downfall of Ma Bâ as believed by the British, it did deny him a major foothold on the south bank and forced him to concentrate his expansionist activity northward into Saloum and Jolof.

RAC   see   ROYAL AFRICAN CORPS

RATE PAYERS ASSOCIATION.   A small Bathurst organization formed in the late 1920s to act as a pressure
group on the British administration.   The influence of
the Rate Payers Association was greatest between 1931
and 1935 when members of the newly created Urban
District Council were normally chosen from its ranks.
Although it continued to have a voice in Banjul affairs
the Association gradually lost its unique position after
the creation of the Bathurst Town Council in 1935.

RECAPTIVES   see   LIBERATED AFRICANS

REEVE, HENRY E.   British writer and Fellow of the Royal
Geographic Society who in 1912 published a book entitled The Gambia.   It remains a good reference work
for some aspects of African migrations and European
occupation.   It is particularly valuable for the section
written by Dr. Hopkinson on animal and plant life in
the Gambia at the beginning of the century.

REFFELL, JOSEPH.   The son of Thomas Reffell, born in
the early 1820s and received his formal education in
Sierra Leone.   He served in the military in the Gambia, but resigned to become a river trader for a European firm.   In the 1860s, accumulated debts forced
him from business.   He then became one of the chief
spokesmen for the younger generation of Liberated
Africans who were openly critical of British administration of the Colony.   He was sent for a legal education to London by Liberated African sponsors.   Although
he did not complete his education, he was a regular
correspondent for the African Times which articulated
the grievances of educated Africans against British rule.
In the early 1870s, Reffell became one of the most
important Gambian leaders in the struggle against Britain's proposal to exchange the Gambia for suitable
French territory elsewhere.   Reffell continued even
after the British decision against exchange in 1876 to
be one of the most outspoken opponents of some of the
oppressive aspects of British rule.   In his later years
he turned to agriculture and attempted to begin a cooperative farming system utilizing modern Western
methods to produce tropical products for export.   He
died in 1886.

REFFELL, THOMAS.  A Christian recaptive Igbo who in the
   1820s was resettled in Bathurst from Sierra Leone.
   His surname was taken from the European manager of
   the Liberated African Department in Sierra Leone.  He
   became a trader and was affluent enough to afford to
   educate his son in Sierra Leone.  He served with distinction in the volunteer militia during the Barra War
   of 1831.  In 1842, he founded the Igbo Society, a
   voluntary paid association open to both men and women
   of Igbo descent.  This was the first of the Friendly
   Societies which became major vehicles for expressing
   to government the opinion of important segments of
   Bathurst society.  Thomas Reffell died in 1849 at the
   age of 55.

RENDALL, GEORGE.  Previously the acting Chief Justice of
   Sierra Leone who was appointed Lieutenant Governor of
   the Gambia in February 1830.  He inherited the pent-
   up resentment of Burungai Sonko, the king of Barra,
   and his advisors.  They felt they had been cheated by
   not receiving payment for the stone quarried at Dog
   Island, resented the cutting back on the king's subsidy,
   and most of all, felt the losses from custom duties
   after the cession of the Ceded Mile.  A minor alterca-
   tion between two men from Essau and the canteen
   operator of Fort Bullen triggered open warfare in
   August 1831.  A motley group of soldiers, merchant
   sailors, and civilians decided to attack the stockaded
   town of Essau.  They were repulsed by the townspeople
   with a number of casualties.  The Europeans fled the
   scene, crossed over to Bathurst, and left Fort Bullen
   to the people of Essau.  Governor Rendall's call for
   assistance was heeded by the French who sent troops
   and a warship.  Their presence stabilized the situation
   near Bathurst.  Burungai Sonko's forces repelled three
   attacks upon Essau, and by the end of the year the
   British had not been able to take the town.  Burungai
   Sonko, however, decided to make peace, and in January
   1832, the Barra War came to an end.  In 1834, Rendall
   was faced with another threat to British supremacy in
   the upper river by the actions of Chief Kemintang.  A
   military expedition was sent against the chief's town of
   Dungasseen.  The British action was a fiasco and they
   had to abandon three of their cannon in their retreat.
   Perhaps the most telling failure of Rendall's tenure
   were the schemes to resettle Liberated Africans in the
   Gambia.  Large numbers were sent from Sierra Leone

without proper advance planning.  Some were sent to
MacCarthy Island, others to the Ceded Mile, and others
were posted outside Bathurst.  With few funds and no
coordination of administrative effort, there was little
Rendall could do to relieve the plight of the majority of
the freed slaves, and it was left to his successor to
solve the problem of the Liberated African.  Rendall
died in 1837 in Bathurst of yellow fever.

RICHARDS, SIR ARTHUR.  Governor of the Gambia from
1933 to 1936 who operated under the handicap of continued reduced revenues due to the depression.  Major
developments during his short tenure were the two
Protectorate Ordinances which clarified the major Protectorate Ordinance of 1933 and established a new yard
tax rate.

RIP   see   BADDIBU

ROWE, SIR SAMUEL.  Army surgeon and Colonial Office administrator posted to West Africa in 1862.  He served
in the Ashanti War of 1873-74 and was then appointed
Administrator of the Gambia where he served from 1875
to 1876.  He was Governor of the West African Settlements (Sierra Leone and the Gambia) from 1876 to 1881,
Governor of Lagos and the Gold Coast from 1881 to
1884, and again Governor of the West African Settlements from 1884 to 1888.  Rowe was a staunch im-
perialist who believed that both Britain and the Africans
would prosper by extension of British rule into the
hinterland.  He opposed the schemes for exchanging the
Gambia, and was an implacable foe of the Colonial Office policy of surrendering to French demands in the
Mellacourie, Porto Novo, and the Gambian interior.  It
was Rowe who planned the expedition of Administrator
Gouldsbury into the upper Gambia.

ROYAL ADVENTURERS OF ENGLAND TRADING INTO
AFRICA.  A company chartered by Charles II to trade
in West Africa.  The glowing reports made by Prince
Rupert were fundamental to the establishment of this
company.  Despite Royal support, particularly from
James, Duke of York, the Adventurers did not find that
trade was very profitable.  The major reasons for lack
of profits were trade losses incurred in the second
Dutch war.  In 1668, the Royal Adventurers sublet their
monopoly to another trading company called the Gambia

Adventurers, and in 1684 relinquished it completely to the Royal African Company.

ROYAL AFRICAN COMPANY.    An English chartered company which assumed a monopoly of trade in West Africa in 1684.    Although the main area of company concern was the Gold Coast, the company did have a considerable investment in the Gambia.    The main base in the Gambia as with previous trading companies was James Island.    The chief factor of the company was in command of a small number of soldiers and an even smaller civilian staff.    In addition to James Island, the company maintained other stations along the river.    The number of these outstations varied, but there normally was trading activity on MacCarthy Island, near Barrakunda Falls, at Bintang, Banyon Point, and Juffure.    At best, the profit levels were low since there were few natural products in the area and the Gambia never was an important slave trading entrepôt.    Health conditions for servants of the company were so poor that the stations were always understaffed and there was a high turn over of personnel.    Far more disasterous to the company were the long series of European wars which pitted France against England.    Local conflict with the French dated from 1681 when they established a trading post at Albreda on the north bank opposite James Island.    A French naval squadron forced abandonment of James Island in 1693, and it was not reoccupied until 1698.    In this year also, Parliament declared the West African trade open to all English merchants.    The Royal African Company was still charged with the upkeep of the trade forts and could level a 10 per cent duty on all goods imported and exported to West Africa.    During the War of Spanish Succession, James Island was plundered by the French in 1704 and 1708.    Only the exhaustion of the rival French company saved the company from further depradations.    The fort on James Island was rebuilt and reoccupied in 1717, but pirates sacked the island, and within four years it was necessary to send a new expedition to restore the fortunes of the company.    An attempt at sending European colonists in the 1720s proved a ghastly failure.    The period between 1730 to 1740 was the most prosperous in the long history of the company.    There was peace in Europe, the slave and gum trade was profitable, and the company received a subsidy from Parliament. The War of Austrian Succession ended this.    Although the English destroyed Albreda, the war disturbed trade, and sickness and death forced the closing of the outstations and near abandonment of James Fort. In 1747, Parliament cancelled the Parliamentary subsidy, and in 1752, the Royal African Company was finally dissolved by Parliamentary action.

ROYAL AFRICAN CORPS (RAC). Formed in 1765 and composed largely of men drawn from the convict hulks in England or military offenders from other regiments, it nevertheless played an important role in the suppression of the slave trade since men of the Corps served not only on land, but also on ships of the West African Patrol. At first it comprised three companies of foot soldiers and was called O'Hara's Corps, named for the first governor of the Senegambia. Men of the Royal African Corps, under the command of Captain Alexander Grant, were responsible for occupying first James Island and then St. Mary's Island in 1816, and they later constructed the barracks and other public buildings in Bathurst. Disease took a frightening toll of the European common soldiers. Between May 1825 and July 1827, 276 of a total of 399 European soldiers landed at Bathurst died. After 1827, all European soldiers in the Gambia were replaced by Africans or West Indian troops.

RUPERT, PRINCE OF THE PALATINATE. A nephew of King Charles I of England, and during the Civil War, one of the king's better generals. He accompanied the future Charles II into exile and took every opportunity of striking at the English Commonwealth government. One such venture concerned the Gambia when Rupert, preying on English commerce, arrived at the estuary of the Gambia River in February 1652. Learning of the presence of three ships of the Commonwealth which had accompanied John Blake on his trading expedition, Rupert sailed upriver to St. Andrew's Island where he received assistance from the Courlander commander. He attacked Blake's ships and captured them, and then sailed from the river northward to Cape Verde where one of his landing parties was captured by the Wolof near Rufisque. Rupert freed his men, but was wounded by an arrow. He then left West Africa for the West Indies. While in the Gambia, Rupert came to believe the reports of huge gold deposits in the hinterland. Later after the restoration, this story played

an important role in the formation of the Royal Adventurers. Prince Rupert was one of the main sponsors and investors in that company.

-S-

SARDU, BAKARI. Ruler of Bondu in the 1860s and 1870s.
He had received a French education, was awarded
the Legion of Honor, and throughout his career was
very careful not to alienate the French. He became
vitally involved with the upper river areas of the Gambia in checking the ambitions of his fellow rulers, and
also for economic gain. In 1866, he led a major invasion through Wuli that briefly threatened MacCarthy
Island. This operation forced the British to abandon
their policy of retreat and to send troops to the island.
In the 1870s, Bakari Sardu formed an unofficial Fulbe
coalition with Alfa Ibrahima of Futa Jallon and Alfa
Molloh. In that period his forces made almost annual
raids into the Gambia. Sardu, depending on the cir-
cumstances, would ally himself either with Soninke or
Marabout factions in the Gambia.

SATIYO-TIYO. Figuratively means owner of the land. He
was the village head, also called at times an alkali.
He was normally the eldest member of a lineage which
was recognized as having titular rights to their office.

SEAGRAM, HENRY F. First Governor of the independent
Colony of the Gambia in 1843, who died of the fever
only a few months after assuming the office and before
he could significantly effect any changes in the Colony.

SEITANE. Wolof term for the devil who can make people
mad and change a normal child into one who is ab-
normal or deformed, and can adversely affect the out-
come of normal decision making.

SELECT COMMITTEE OF PARLIAMENT (1842). Created
primarily as a response to the activities of George
MacLean, the company administrator in the Gold Coast.
The Committee called into question the methodology of
British government in all the West African areas. As
a result of its recommendations, the Crown assumed
direct control over the Gold Coast and the decision was
taken to allow each British territory to have its own

administration without reference to a governor-in-chief.
The first governor of the Gambia under these new regulations was Captain H. F. Seagram.

SELECT COMMITTEE OF PARLIAMENT (1865). Created
because of Parliamentary pressure to reduce the cost
of administering the Empire. The Committee based its
recommendations largely upon the report of Colonel
H. St. George Ord. It enunciated the doctrine of no
territorial expansion in Africa which remained the dominant Colonial philosophy for over twenty years. The
Colonial Office, following the report of the Committee,
ordered the abandonment of MacCarthy Island. British
presence in the vicinity of MacCarthy Island was left
to a factor who was also a trader in the upper river
areas. He had no official authority and had to operate
without benefit of British troops. More important for
the Gambia, the Select Committee recommended that
all British West African possessions be placed once
again under the direct control of a governor-in-chief,
resident in Freetown. This was effected by 1866. In
1874, Lagos and the Gold Coast were removed from
such control, but the Gambia remained under such control until 1888. The chief executive officer resident
in the Gambia was called an Administrator.

SENEGAL COMPANY. A short lived, but important commercial company established by the French in 1672 as
a successor to Colbert's grandiose West Indies Company. In 1677, a French fleet captured Goree from
the Dutch, and this became the main base of operations
for the company. In the next few years, the company,
in conjunction with French naval vessels, harassed
the shipping of the Royal African Company and attempted
to supplant the English on the Gambia River. Factors
were established at a number of locales south of Cape
Verde, a punitive expedition was mounted against
Saloum, and in 1681, the first trading station at Albreda was built opposite James Island. The outbreak
of war in 1689 reversed the fortunes of the company,
and they gave up their monopoly first to the Guinea
Company, and finally in 1696 to the Royal Senegal Company.

SENEGAMBIA, PROVINCE OF. During the Seven Years War,
the British occupied and garrisoned the Senegambia. At
the conclusion of the war, administration of the area was

vested in a Committee of Merchants. Revived French
activity and the weakness of the company caused a re-
version of the territory to the Crown in 1765 under the
name Province of the Senegambia. The government
system was based on that of an American colony with
a Governor, Council, and Chief Justice. The first
governor was Colonel O'Hara who also commanded
three companies of troops known as O'Hara's Corps,
but later renamed the Royal African Corps. O'Hara's
11-year tenure of office was marked by continued difficulties with French traders on the Gambia River and
even more vexing problems of controlling the actions
of the lieutenant-governors and their troops at James
Island. Matthias MacNamara, who had exercised almost independent command in the Gambia, succeeded
O'Hara as governor and almost immediately became
embroiled with Captain Wall, his lieutenant in the Gambia. This struggle, which culminated in MacNamara's
removal, weakened the entire government of the province at a time when the French had decided to aid the
American Revolution. MacNamara's successor,
Governor Clarke, died in August 1778, and only an
ensign was in command at St. Louis in January 1779
when a French fleet appeared and seized the station.
The following month, the French forced the surrender
of James Island and razed the fort there. Later in
the year, a British squadron occupied Goree, but found
James Fort to be in no condition to be assigned as a
garrison and no further attempts were made to occupy
any territory in the Gambia during the war. The
Treaty of Versailles in 1783 returned all of the Province of Senegambia to France with the exception of the
Gambia River and James Island, which were retained
by the British.

SERAHULI. Inhabitants of part of the area which once was
the ancient kingdom of Wuli. Today they form the
largest population block in the extreme upper river
areas of the Gambia. They are mixtures of Mandingo,
Berber, and Fulbe. They are primarily farmers,
handicapped more than other peoples of the Gambia because of the poorness of the soil. The Serahuli have
in the past suffered greatly from food shortages, and
the hungry season was an ever-present factor in their
lives until the close of the 1950s. In the course of the
Soninke-Marabout Wars of the 19th century, many Serahuli became mercenaries willing to serve in the armies
of either side.

SERER. According to their traditions, they were an agricultural people who resided in Futa Toro when a series
of invasions by the Fulbe drove them southward. Long
association with Wolof, Fulbe, and Mandingo has produced a complex racial admixture of the Serer. The Serer
speak a language classified by Joseph H. Greenberg as a
part of the northern sub-group of the Niger-Kordofanian
family and is closely akin to Paolar, the language of
the Fulbe and Tucolor. The bulk of the nearly one-
half million Serer live in the Sine and Saloum areas of
Senegal. Two neighboring peoples, the Serer N'Dieg-
hem and the Niominka, are considered branches of the
Serer although they speak different dialects and had
more simplified political systems. The main group of
Serer were referred to by early European travellers
as "Barbesins" meaning people of the Bur Sine. After
the mid-19th century the two Serer kingdoms occupied
very strategic locations, blocking southward expansion
of the French and also the ambitions of Ma Bâ of
Baddibu. In both states, peanut cultivation became
very important for the Serer peasants as well as the
French merchants. The Serer had a complex social
and political organization in each of their two kingdoms.
The burs or kings, chosen from the guelowar (matrilineage of the Mandingo founders of their states), secure
in the prosperity of their farming villages, could command very large armies (tyeddos). The Bur Sine and
the Sine tyeddo were responsible for the defeat and
death of Ma Bâ in 1867 which ended all chances for
a unified Muslim polity in the Senegambia. The Serer
population in the Gambia is very small, numbering
under 10,000 persons.

SEYFU (pl. Seyfolu). Mandingo word meaning chief or ruler.
This was the title used by the British for all the 35
chiefs of the modern Protectorate.

SILLA, FODI. Emerged in the early 1870s as the leader of
the Marabout forces in Kombo. By 1874, the Marabouts had taken Brikama and most of the major towns
in eastern Kombo. Many Soninke fled to safety in
British Kombo and some, using this as a place of sanctuary, raided into Marabout territory. Because of the
inherent danger in this to British Kombo, Sir Cornelius
Kortright, the Administrator, in 1874 concluded a treaty
with Fodi Silla which created a neutral zone between
Yundum and British territory. The arrangements were

violated by both Soninke and Marabouts, and in the following year, Fodi Silla's forces were everywhere vic-
torious over those of the king of Kombo, Tomani Bojang.   The king was forced to retreat to Lamin, a town
within a few yards of the border of British Kombo.
The rainy season prevented open warfare between Fodi
Silla and the British.   Tomani Bojang, receiving no
direct assistance from the British, capitulated in September 1875, and agreed to become a Muslim.   Fodi
Silla then allowed him and his people to continue to
live in Kombo.   Fodi Silla then became the dominant
factor in all of the Kombo, having established good relations with his neighbor and fellow Marabout leader,
Fodi Kabba.   Except for his slave raiding activities,
he caused the British administrators little trouble until
the joint Anglo-French Boundary Commission arrived
in his territory in 1891.   Understandably outraged at
the implications of the Franco-British Convention of
1889, both Fodi Silla and Fodi Kabba attempted to interfere with the work of the Commissioners.   Subsequently
three gunboats were stationed near the areas where the
Commission was working.   This show of force and the
military actions taken against Fodi Kabba in Foni,
Kiang, and Jarra, caused Fodi Silla to remain relatively quiet in 1892.   The British recognized him as
chief of Western Kombo and paid him a stipend.   Minor
problems related to Bathurst based traders in his territory and his attitude toward the slave trade caused
the British in February 1894 to mount a two-pronged
offensive against him.   After initial failures, the British
West Indian troops took Gunjur and forced Fodi Silla to
flee to Foni.   The Jola leaders there refused him sanctuary, and he and his followers retreated to the Casamance.   There his followers were disarmed by the
French.   Fodi Silla was deported to St. Louis and later
died in exile.

SIMOTTO MORO.   A Torodo Fulbe, a Muslim teacher, and
a resident in Fuladu in the 1860s who had gathered
around him a group of disciples.   He appeared to Alfa
and Musa Molloh as a threat to their complete control
of Fuladu.   Before they could act against him, he
moved with his followers across the Gambia River to
Wuli and there established the heavily fortified town of
Toubacouta which in a short time became a center for
trade and learning in the upper river area.   Disaffected
Fulbe from Fuladu reinforced Simotto Moro's power,

and until his death in 1881, Toubacouta was safe from
attack from Fuladu.

SINGHATEH, ALHAJI FARIMANG MAMADI.   The first Gam-
bian-born Governor of the Gambia, succeeding Sir John
Paul in December 1965.   He was born at Georgetown
in 1912 of an old Mandingo family, but was later
adopted by a British District Officer who helped educate him at local primary schools and at Armitage.
Beginning in 1935, he was associated with the Medical
Department.   He qualified as a pharmacist in 1950,
and after retiring from the Civil Service in 1963,
operated his own pharmacy at Farafenni.   He had been
Chairman of the Protectorate Welfare Societies before
becoming associated with the People's Progressive
Party which he supported although he was never politically active.   He was appointed a member of the Public
Service Commission in 1964, the highest position held
before his appointment as Governor.

SISAY, SHERIF.   Politician, born in 1935 at Kudag in the
Protectorate, one of the children of Sekuba Sisay,
chief of Niamina District from 1927 to 1952.   He was
educated in Koranic schools and spent eight years at
the Secondary School in Georgetown.   In 1957, he became a clerk in the Education Department, and was
a founder member of the People's Progressive Party.
He became its first Secretary-General in 1959, a post
he held until he broke with the party in 1968.   In the
1960 elections, he was one of the nine PPP members
elected to the House of Assembly, and he was appointed
a minister without portfolio in the Executive Council.
In March 1961, with the other PPP members, he resigned because the governor appointed P. S. N'Jie of
the United Party as Chief Minister.   However, the
1962 elections gave the PPP a definitive majority, and
Sisay became the Finance Minister and was normally
recognized as the number two man in the government.
As Finance Minister, Sisay framed a series of budgets
which reflected Gambia's modest economic position,
but which did allow for needed development and growth.
In September 1968, after some disagreement with the
other leaders of the PPP, Sisay and three other young
politicians were expelled from the party.   In October,
he was instrumental in forming a new political vehicle,
the People's Progressive Alliance (PPA), which joined
the United Party in opposition.   The PPA vehemently

opposed the government's proposal for a Republic until
just before the April 1970 plebiscite when the party
leaders reversed themselves.   The fortunes of Sisay
and the PPA declined rapidly after 1970.

SITWELL, F. C.   Appointed the first Travelling Commissioner for the south bank areas of the Protectorate in
January 1893.   He was thus the first permanent British
official in all the troubled areas from Kombo to Niamina.   With his partner, J. H. Ozanne, the north bank
Commissioner, he represented the Crown to the peoples
of approximately 150 miles of riverine territory.   Since
he had no military or police escort, he had to be very
diplomatic in informing the chiefs and the people of
their new status and of the laws and ordinances of the
Colony which applied to them.   He also tried to act as
a neutral judge in any dispute which arose between villages or chiefdoms.   Although more Travelling Commissioners were appointed in the late 1890s, their tasks
were made even more difficult by the enactment of the
Protectorate Ordinance of 1894, the Yard Tax Ordinance,
and the Public Lands Ordinance of 1897.   In 1899, a
long-standing dispute over rice land flared between the
Soninkes of Jataba and the Marabouts of Sankandi.   Sitwell adjudicated the matter and decided in favor of
Jataba.   The Marabouts of Sankandi, mostly followers
of Fodi Kabba, refused to abide by the decision.   Sitwell, accompanied by his replacement, F. E. Silva, 11
African constables, and Mansa Koto, the chief of Battelling, proceeded to Sankandi in early 1900 to enforce the
land decision.   After a brief discussion, Sitwell's group
proceeded to the center of the town, an argument developed, and some of the Marabouts opened fire.   Sitwell, Silva, Mansa Koto, and six constables were killed.
The violence done to Sitwell's party convinced both the
British and French governments that the interior regions
had to be pacified and led to the joint military expedition of 1901.

SLAVE TRADE.   Slavery was an indigenous institution among
all the peoples of the Gambia.   It was converted by the
Atlantic slave trade into a mutually profitable business
for both Africans and Europeans.   The Portuguese in
their earliest voyages captured slaves, but slave-trading
did not become important until the 16th century with
the development of plantation economies in the Western
Hemisphere.   The earliest English and French traders

to the Gambia were more concerned with gum, gold,
and ivory, and Richard Jobson in the 17th century in-
dignantly refused to trade in slaves.   However, by the
18th century, traffic in slaves was the most important
business of the Royal African Company.   Even then the
Gambia was not considered a good recruiting area,
most of the trading being done along the Gold Coast,
Dahomey, and western Nigeria.   There are no reliable
figures for the numbers transported from the Gambia.
In peak years perhaps as many as 2000 were sold, but
according to Moore, the average during the first quarter
of the 18th century was 1000 per year.   British abolition in 1807 dealt a major blow to the slave trade, but
slave ships continued to operate in the Gambia region
for decades afterward, and individual rulers such as
Fodi Kabba continued to pursue the practice throughout
the 19th century.   One of the major reasons for the
occupation of Bathurst (Banjul) was the British desire
to block the trade in slaves from the Gambia River.

SMALL, EDWARD.   Journalist, labor leader, and politician,
educated in Bathurst.   In 1922 he founded the earliest
influential Gambian newspaper, The Gambia Outlook,
first published in Dakar because Small had no press.
He was one of the first Gambians to think in nationalist
and Pan-African terms and with Casley-Hayford of the
Gold Coast was one of the organizers of the West African National Congress movement in the 1920s.   In 1929,
he founded the Bathurst-based Gambia Labor Union, and
in that year led a successful strike of artisans and
river craft workers.   The union continued to be weak,
primarily because of government attitudes, but it remained, for over two decades, the only attempt to
organize Gambian workers.   Small's activities were
mainly responsible for the important Gambia Trade
Union Ordinance of 1932.   He was nominated for a seat
on the general executive council of the International
Confederation of Free Trade Unions, and held that position from 1945 until his death in January 1957.   In the
early 1930s, Small helped organize, and became the
Chairman of, the Rate Payers' Association which always
returned candidates to the Urban District Council.   He
was nominated to the Legislative Council in the early
1940s and won election to a seat on that body in 1947.
In 1951, he was defeated for reelection by I. M. Garba-
Jahumpa and J. C. Faye.

SOLDIER TOWN.  A section of Banjul (Bathurst) lying south-
east of Albion Place.  This was the area where most
of the discharged soldiers resided in the early 19th
century.

SONINKE.  A term which literally means giver of libations.
In the upper Senegal River area, it is a name given to
a people who are also called Sarakolle by the French
and Serahuli by the British.  It is also a term applied
to the ancient rulers of the West African empire of
Ghana.  In the Gambia in the 19th century, this term
applied to the traditionalist faction in the religious conflicts of the 19th century.  To the Marabouts, the term
had similar perjorative connotations as that of the term
Kaffir to South Africans.

SONINKE-MARABOUT WARS.  A series of conflicts which
began in the mid-1850s between Islamic converts and
those Gambian leaders representing traditional political
and religious interests.  At one time or another, these
conflicts affected all of the riverine areas of the Gambia.  The most significant long range effects of the
wars was the destruction of most of the older Mandingo
polities and the creation of new states, and the conversion of most of the Gambian population to Islam.
The wars peaked in the two decades after 1860 with the
conquests of Ma Bâ, Alfa Molloh, and Fodi Kabba.
They did not officially end until the death of Fodi Kabba
in 1901.  (For further details of the Soninke-Marabout
Wars, see MOLLOH, ALFA; MOLLOH, MUSA; BÂ;
KABBA; SILLA; SONKO; D'ARCY; O'CONNOR.)

SONKO, BURUNGAI.  Became the ruler of Barra in 1823,
and three years later signed a convention with Alexander
Grant giving the British control of the Ceded Mile, upon
which they constructed Fort Bullen.  During the next
five years, the king came to regret the loss of his customs revenues, and pressured by under chiefs, adopted
an anti-British attitude.  Because of actions against
Bathurst traders in Niumi, the British suspended their
annual payments to him.  His attitude and the foolish-
ness of European and African traders in Bathurst led
to the Barra War.  A slight incident in August 1831,
between two intoxicated subjects of the king and the
canteen keeper at Fort Bullen, led to an attempt to
take Essau by a motley assortment of Bathurst citizens
and soldiers.  They were repulsed with severe losses,

and the British abandoned Barra to the king.  Governor
Rendall, fearing collaboration between Sonko and the
king of Kombo, pleaded for assistance from the French
at Goree.  With French help, a further futile attempt
was made to take Essau.  Later, even after reinforcements had arrived from Sierra Leone, the British were
unable to capture the town.  The king's subjects had,
nevertheless, suffered heavily from the war, and Burungai Sonko made peace in January 1832, reconfirming
the Ceded Mile Treaty.

SOUTHORN, LADY BELLA.  Sister of Leonard Woolf and
sister-in-law of the novelist Virginia Woolf, and wife
of Governor Sir Wilfred Thomas Southorn.  Lady
Southorn was also an author of considerable distinction
who wrote many articles concerning the Gambia.  In
1952 she published an interesting, informative extended
essay on Gambian history, society, and politics entitled The Gambia:  The Story of the Groundnut Colony.

SOUTHORN, SIR WILFRED THOMAS.  Governor of the Gambia from 1936 to 1942.  Any plans he had for major
improvements either for the Colony or the Protectorate
had to be framed within the context of revenues expected from an economically non-viable area still re-
covering from the depression.  After 1939, the economy
of the Gambia improved substantially as the Gambia
became an important staging area during World War II.
The period between 1940 and 1942 was particularly tense
because the Gambia was surrounded on three sides by
Senegal whose government was controlled by Vichy
France.

SPEER, FRANCIS.  A minor merchant in the Gambia who had
come to the territory as a doctor in 1876.  In 1879, he
had lengthy conversations with the French chargé d'af-
faire in London concerning reopening discussions on an
exchange of the Gambia.  The French were led to believe that Speer was a spokesman for the Bathurst
merchants, and he reported that they were only concerned with making a profit from their investments.
Within a short time, Speer's real position became known
and the French did not at that time officially present any
proposals to the British Government.

STIBBS, BARTHOLOMEW (Captain).  Sent to the Gambia by
the Royal African Company in 1723 with the specific

purpose of searching for the legendary upriver gold
mines mentioned by Prince Rupert and Vermuyden.
He reached Barrakunda Falls in February 1724, and
proceeded approximately sixty miles above them before
turning back.  Stibbs reported that he found no minerals
and considered Vermuyden's report to be a myth.  His
negative report discouraged the company from further
exploration.  Captain Stibbs' expedition has been recorded in Frances Moore's Travels into the Inland
Parts of Africa.  Stibbs later returned to the Gambia
as a merchant of the company and had a role in the
affairs of 1729-30 when some of the disaffected Europeans on James Island threatened to revolt and blow up
the fort.

STIEL, OTTO.  The third chief agent of Courland in the
      Gambia.  He was appointed in 1653 and spent six years
      in the area trying to improve trade and diplomatic re-
      lations with the mid-river Gambians.  However, his
      successes were compromised by European disturbances.
      Courlander ships were seized by both the Dutch and the
      English in their commercial war.  The Dutch at Goree
      did not wish trade competition in the Senegambia from
      interlopers, and twice captured the fort on St. Andrew's
      Island and Stiel was made prisoner each time.  His
      release was forced the first time by the actions of a
      French privateer in Swedish employ and the second time by
      forces loyal to the king of Barra.  The capture of James,
      Duke of Courland, by the Swedes following a dynastic
      dispute, and the subsequent agreement reached by Cour-
      land and England in 1664 which ceded St. Andrew's Is-
      land, undercut all of Stiel's work in the Gambia.

STONE CIRCLES.  Megaliths still of unknown origin found
      in western Africa from the southern Sahara in the north
      to Guinea-Bissau in the south.  Most of them are lo-
      cated in Senegal.  All except two of the circles in the
      Gambia are on the north bank.  They are composed of
      between 10 and 20 standing laterite stones which vary
      in height from two to eight feet.  These stones are
      arranged in circles between 10 and 20 feet in diameter.
      In some locales there is a complex of circles.  Wassu
      has 11 circles and Ker-Batch has nine.  The stones
      were cut from neighboring hillsides and some of the
      larger stones weigh as much as 10 tons.  Their trans-
      portation to the circle sites involved a considerable
      labor force and complex organization.  Professional and

amateur excavations indicate that the area within some
of the circles was used as a burial place. Some skele-
tons and many artifacts have been uncovered. Present-
day Gambians in the vicinity of the circles have no
clear notion of their origin or use. The best specula-
tion of professionals is that the circles belong to the
pre-Islamic period, perhaps as early as the 13th century, and were constructed by either the Jola, Serer,
or Mandingo people.

STRANGE FARMERS.  Landless men who migrated seasonally
to the Gambia to help with planting and harvesting crops.
During the Soninke-Marabout Wars, they served the additional function of mercenaries. During the 20th century, the strange farmers would make their own contracts with village headmen and be assigned to work for
specific farmers in a village. They were assigned
portions of land to work for themselves in their free
time, and would also normally be required to grow a
part of the additional food supply needed for their sustenance. The pressure upon available food supplies in
the Gambia after 1945 caused the Colonial government
and the chiefs to take steps to limit the immigration of
these foreigners into the Gambia.

SUMA.  Among the Mandingo kingdoms, certain village leaders
had more authority over a larger area of land than other
alkali.  These lineage leaders were called suma.  In
Baddibu, Jarra, Niumi, Kiang, and Kombo, the kingship
rotated between certain lineages with the suma of a particular lineage becoming the mansa or king.

SUMAKUNDA.  The lineage in direct line of succession to the
kingship in Mandingo kingdoms.

-T-

TALL, AL HAJJ UMAR.  The khalifa of the Tijaniyya tariq
in the western Sudan, born about 1790, educated in the
Futa Toro, and later travelled widely including a five-
year pilgrimage to Mecca.  In North Africa, he came
under the influence of Ahmad al Tijani whose teachings
stressed the special place in paradise reserved by Allah
for the faithful.  Umar later lived in Hausaland where
he married one of the daughters of Sultan Bello of So-
koto.  In 1838, he left Hausaland and established a

religious and military base at Dinguiray. By 1852 his
following was large enough to declare a jihad against
the Bambara, and he conquered Kaarta. In the decade
after 1852, Umar's followers conquered Segu and Macina, and gained control of the upper Senegal River
area. In 1863, Umar's prestige was at its zenith with
the capture of Timbuktu. In the same year he was
killed suppressing a revolt in Macina. He bequeathed
a huge but heterogeneous empire to his son, Ahmadu.
Umar's teaching and example of conquering the territories of unbelievers had a great influence upon Muslim
teachers in the Senegambia. Ma Bâ and Alfa Molloh
both had direct connections with the Tijaniyya movement.

TANCROWALL. A Portuguese settlement sited in the locale
of the modern village of Tankular. There was a church
with priest in residence there as late as 1730. The
Royal African Company briefly had a factory at Tancrowall in the 1730s.

TARIQ. A subdivision of Islam comprising those individuals
who subscribe to a common philosophy and ritual. The
two most celebrated tariq brotherhoods in West Africa
were the Qadiriyya, reflecting the attitudes of the more
conservative Muslim teachers, and the Tijaniyya,
founded in 1781, which demanded of its followers more
puritanical personal and social attitudes. The Tijaniyya
was particularly important in the Senegambia during the
latter 19th century in destroying the power of the older
"pagan" dynasties.

THOMAS, G. J. (Sergeant). Policeman and administrator.
He was sent by Administrator Carter to Baddibu in 1885
to attempt to bring an end to the fighting between the
forces of Mamadou N'Dare, Saër Maty, and Biram
Cisse. In 1889, he was appointed manager of British
Kombo and later took part in the Tonataba expedition
of 1892 and that of Sankandi in 1901. He retired in
1903 and died in 1935.

THOMPSON, GEORGE. Explorer and servant of the British
Guinea Company sent to the Gambia River in 1618.
Despite the massacre of a number of his men by the
Portuguese, Thompson was optimistic that contact with
the upper river would produce a wealth of gold. In
1619, with a few companions, he reached Tenda above
Barrakunda Falls. Thompson wanted to proceed further

into the hinterland, but his associates refused.  In the
ensuing quarrel, Thompson was killed.  All of his discoveries and observations perished with him since he
had committed nothing to writing.  It was left for
Richard Jobson the following year to retrace Thompson's
journey and record his findings for his superiors in
London.

TIJANIYYA.  A Muslim tariq or voluntary brotherhood,
    founded in the late 18th century in North Africa.  It
    was more democratic than other tariqs, imposed fewer
    obligations on the believers, and was simple to under-
    stand.  It was also much more puritanical and the
    members came to view themselves as an elite group
    within Islam.  The most important of the Tijaniyya
    leaders in the Senegambia was Al Hajj Umar, the
    khalifa of the western Sudan who in the decade after
    1850 created a large, heterogenous empire which
    stretched from the middle Senegal River area past
    Timbuktu.  Tijaniyya teachers were at the forefront
    of the Soninke-Marabout disturbances in the Gambia.
    Ma Bâ of Baddibu and Alfa Molloh both had Tijaniyya
    connections.

TOMANI.  One of the nine Mandingo kingdoms located along
    the south bank of the Gambia River in the early 19th
    century.  It stretched from a point opposite Sami Creek
    to Tubakuta.  The Mandingo ruling dynasty was over-
    thrown by Alfa Molloh in the late 1860s and was in-
    corporated into the new state of Fuladu.  In the 20th
    century reorganization of Gambian chiefdoms, the
    area which was Tomani became the District of Fuladu
    East.

TORDO FULBE.  A dialect group of the Fulbe related to
    their occupation as scholars.  Although fewer in number
    than the other Fulbe groups, they had profound impact
    on the history of the upper Gambia since most Torodo
    were Muslims and their inherent position gave them the
    opportunity to influence other Muslim groups at the be-
    ginning of the Soninke-Marabout conflicts.

TREGASKIS, THE REV. BENJAMIN.  Superintendent of the
    Wesleyan Mission in Sierra Leone and the Gambia from
    1864 to 1870.  He held a district meeting in early 1871
    in Bathurst which passed a resolution condemning any
    transfer of the Gambia to France, thus joining the

Wesleyans with the bulk of the business community in
opposition to Colonial Office policy.

TYEDDO. Warriors in service to a Wolof or Serer king or
chief who were selected from the jam or slave class.
They were also known as slaves of the crown.


-U-


UNITED PARTY (UP). Formed in October 1951, after the
failure of Pierre Sarr N'Jie, a Bathurst barrister, to
be elected to the Legislative Council. The United Party
was a party which from the first showed great strength
in the Colony area, particularly among the Wolof. The
party was successful in returning N'Jie to the Legislative Council at the head of the poll in the elections of
1954. The following year, N'Jie disagreed with the
governor and resigned from the government. The UP
thus escaped the stigma attached to the older parties
of being tools of the British administration. In the
election of 1960 when the franchise was extended to
the Protectorate, the UP elected six members to the
House of Representatives. The newly created People's
Progressive Party proved to have more popular support
in the Protectorate, returning eight members. However, in 1961, the British governor turned to N'Jie to
be the new Chief Minister, and until the elections of
1962, the UP, in liaison with the Protectorate chiefs,
controlled the government. The new Constitution under
which the 1962 elections were held reduced the chiefs'
power to only a nominal degree, and the UP won only
13 seats to the House of Representatives as compared
to 18 for the PPP. The influence of the UP after Gambian independence in 1965 continued to decline. In the
elections of 1966, despite a coalition with the Congress
Party, the UP could win only Colony seats while the
PPP won 24 Protectorate seats. The UP became deeply
divided over policy, and in May 1970, P. S. N'Jie was
removed as the party leader and replaced by his brother,
Ebrimah Dowda N'Jie. On the death of E. D., the
party's councils once more selected P. S. as leader.
The lowest point in the fortunes of the UP came when
the House of Representatives removed P. S. N'Jie from
its roster because of non-attendance.

USIDIMARE, ANTONIOTTO. A Genoese sea captain in the

employ of the Portuguese. In 1455, he was commissioned by Prince Henry to explore the coastline south
of Cape Verde. In early 1456, he was joined off Cape
Verde by the ship commanded by Alvise da Cadamosto.
The two explorers led the first European explorations
of the estuary of the Gambia River. In a second exploration, they were escorted inland approximately 60
miles, and spent over two weeks conversing and trading
with Gambian rulers. Leaving the Gambia River, Usidimare proceeded to sail southward as far south as
Cape Mesurado before returning to Portugal.

USTICK, STEPHEN. A factor assigned to James Island by
Major Robert Holmes in 1661. Left in command of 29
men in the fort, he twice resisted the attempts of
Peter Justobaque, chief factor of the Dutch West Indies
Company, to seize all the recently acquired British
strongholds in the Gambia.

-V-

VALENTINE, LOUIS FRANCIS. A civil servant and High
Commissioner to Britain, born in 1908 in Bathurst.
He was educated at Methodist Boys High School and
later Fourah Bay College where he received a B. A.
in 1930. Three years later he entered the Civil
Service and became a senior administrator in 1949,
serving in a number of departments. In 1960, he was
appointed Postmaster-General and two years later became the first Gambian Chairman of the Public Service
Commission. He was Joint Secretary of the Senegal-
Gambian Inter-Ministerial Commission in 1961. He
became the first Gambian High Commissioner in February 1965.

VAN DER PLAS, CHARLES OLKE. Dutch administrator,
United Nations official, and creator and head of the
Gambian Department of Community Development. He
first came to the Gambia in 1954 to make a survey of
Gambian economic and political problems for the United
Nations. He returned to the Gambia in 1963 and con-
vinced the government to establish the Department of
Community Development with minimal financing, and he
established his headquarters at Massembi.

VERMUYDEN, JOHN (Colonel). A servant of the Royal

Adventurers who in December 1661 left Elephant Island
on an extended exploration of the upper river areas.
His later report claimed that his expedition penetrated
further into the interior than had Jobson.  He claimed
to have passed Jobson's Tenda, the confluence of the
Neriko River, and to have reached beyond the Niololo-
koba River before being halted in April 1662 by rapids.
Vermuyden reported that at this point he had discovered
a great amount of gold.  He told Prince Rupert of this
discovery and explained that he did not bring out great
quantities for fear of his companions.  In 1725, Captain
Stibbs retraced Vermuyden's journey without discovering
the slightest indication of the fabled gold deposits.

-W-

WALL, JOSEPH (Captain).   An Irishman who had served in
the Royal Marines and in the East India Company forces
before joining O'Hara's Corps in the Senegambia in 1773.
After O'Hara's departure in late 1775, Wall served
briefly as Governor of the Senegambia until displaced
by Matthias MacNamara.   He was then posted to James
Island as Lieutenant-Governor of the Gambia where his
independent actions and harsh rule caused difficulty with
the garrison.   He was ordered imprisoned by Mac-
Namara and spent 10 months in confinement in James
Fort before being brought to trial.   In a celebrated
case in 1777, Governor MacNamara's allegations
against Wall were dismissed and subsequently Wall
won two civil cases against the Governor and the Council of Trade dismissed MacNamara.   Wall returned to
the Senegambia and later, while Governor at Goree,
had three soldiers flogged to death.   He fled to Europe,
and 20 years later was captured, tried for murder, and
executed.

WALLIKUNDA RICE SCHEME.   An attempt on the part of
the Colonial Development Corporation to utilize modern
technology to develop 3400 acres and grow irrigated
rice profitably.   In the early 1950s, the corporation
sent over 60 construction workers complege with drag
lines and bulldozers to construct irrigation channels,
sluices, and a pumping station at Wallikunda.   Only
200 acres were ever planted and the yield was very
low, no more than by using the traditional methods.
The corporation abandoned the scheme in 1954 except

for a small portion of the land which was retained as
an experimental station. This ill-conceived venture was
even more expensive than the Yundum egg fiasco and
cost the corporation £1,115,000.

WESLEYAN MISSION. Its activities in the Gambia date from
February 1821, when John Morgan and his wife arrived
from England. The first attempt at establishing a station at Mandinari in Kombo was a failure, but the work
of an expanded staff in Bathurst was a success. A
mission house and school were started in 1825, and in
1834, the present Wesleyan Church was built for the
250-member congregation. In 1838, the Wesleyans
took over 600 acres of land on MacCarthy Island and
began a model farm and agricultural school there. In
the early 19th century, the Wesleyans were particularly
effective working with Liberated Africans. Much of the
responsibility for education in the Colony and Protectorate in the early 20th century was assumed by the Wesleyans. In addition to primary schools in Bathurst,
they operated a Girls High School and a Boys High
School, and were involved after 1947 in helping to
operate the Bathurst School of Science. In the late
1950s, the two Methodist High Schools were joined to
form the present Bathurst High School.

WEST AFRICAN FIELD FORCE. In 1958 Governor Wyn
Harris and his advisors seeking to economize phased
out "A" company of the Sierra Leone Battalion. In
March the government created the West African Field
Force using the officers and men from the old company.
The Field Force became a part of the regular police
in the Gambia, comprising in the 1960's approximately
140 men or roughly one-quarter of the entire police
force. Men of the Field Force still continued to be
quartered in their old barracks at Fajara. The force
was used primarily for ceremonial functions and as
shock troops to provide for the security of the capital.

WEST INDIES COMPANY (Dutch). Created by the States
General in 1617 and organized according to Chambers
reflecting the ambitions of the great maritime cities
of Holland. In 1621, the company obtained the Island
of Goree for its base of operations to challenge French
supremacy in Senegambian trade. The company almost
annually sent small ships from Goree to trade along
the Gambia River, but the profit for such ventures was

quite low.  In the 1650s, the company at first cooperated with the Duke of Courland in his Gambia trading
venture, but by 1660 they had seized St. Andrew's Island from him.  Although the island was given back to
the Duke's representatives, it was obvious that the
Dutch intended to have it as a base for their Gambian
operations.  They were forestalled in this by the actions
of Captain Robert Holmes of the English Royal Adventurers, whose forces took the island in March 1661 and
renamed it James Island.  Holmes, in charge of another expedition, captured Goree from the Dutch in early
1664, but this station was lost later in the year when
the Dutch Admiral de Ruyter in command of 13 ships
arrived in West Africa.  De Ruyter, however, by-passed
the English possessions in the Gambia.  The Dutch company thereafter enjoyed a decade of relative supremacy
in the Senegal region.  However, the onset of the
French Wars in Europe ended the Dutch interlude in
Senegambia.  In 1677, the French Admiral d'Entrées
captured Goree and then drove the Dutch from all their
coastal factories.  After this, the Dutch company never
attempted to challenge France or Britain in the Senegambia.

WEST INDIES COMPANY (French).  A short-lived company
created in 1664 by the all-powerful Minister Colbert.
In a grandiose gesture, he gave the company monopo-
listic rights along the shores of the Atlantic Ocean
from Canada to the Cape of Good Hope.  His scheme
for wresting trade from the enemies of France by
means of this company collapsed in 1672.  Trading
rights in West Africa were then assigned to the Senegal
Company.

WINDLEY, SIR EDWARD.  Governor of the Gambia from 1957
to 1962.  He was responsible for introducing the new
Constitution which provided for a greatly expanded House
of Assembly and allowed the elective principle to be applied to the Protectorate in 1960.  He made the decision
to appoint Gambians to ministerial positions in the government based upon the results of the election, and in
1961 appointed P. S. N'Jie, leader of the United Party,
as Chief Minister.

WOLOF.  One of the most important people of the Senegambia.  They comprise a population in Senegal estimated
to be over three quarters of a million persons with

heaviest concentrations in Walo, Cayor, Jolof, and
parts of Baol, Sine, and Saloum.   In the Gambia,
there are approximately 40,000 found mainly in upper
and lower Saloum districts and in the northern sections
of Niani, Sami, Niumi, Jokadu, and also restricted
areas of upper Baddibu.   Banjul (Bathurst) is also pre-
dominantly a Wolof town, but these have a different
origin than those of the Protectorate since their an-
cestors came from the area of Dakar immediately after
the founding of Bathurst.   The Wolof language has been
classified by Joseph H. Greenberg as a part of the northern
sub-group of the Niger-Kordofanian family of languages,
and is a commercial language spoken beyond the
boundaries of the Senegambia.   Wolof social organization is extremely complex, based upon a tripartite
division of the society into the freeborn, low-caste
persons, and slaves.   Although many modern-day Wolof
are involved in trading and a variety of tasks associated with modern urban life, most Wolof are agricul-
turalists and live in villages.   The land is divided into
small plots assigned to individuals who practice sub-
sistance agriculture.   Their major cash crop in both
Senegal and the Gambia is groundnuts (peanuts).   Historically the Wolof states of the Senegambia were Jolof,
Walo, Baol, and Cayor whose rulers (burba, temy, or
damel) controlled their people through a complex bureaucracy combined with armed force.   Those kingdoms
played an important role in temporarily checking the
southward and eastward advance of the French in the
two decades after 1855, but were among the first territories incorporated into the French empire during the
"scramble."   The Wolof in the area of the Gambia
Protectorate had not established strong central polities
before the Soninke-Marabout Wars and were politically
dependent upon Mandingo or Serer overlords.

WRIGHT, SIR ANDREW B.   Governor of the Gambia from
1947 to 1949.   Although he was not involved in the
planning, the Colonial Development Corporation made
and implemented its decision to invest in the disasterous
Yundum egg scheme and the marginal experimental rice
farm at Wallikunda during his tenure of office.   He also
had to frame his budgets with the knowledge that much
of the financing for continued improvements in the economic and social sphere envisioned by the British
government in the period immediately after World War
II would not be forthcoming.

WULI. Located in the extreme upper river area, it was in the 19th century one of the five north bank kingdoms controlled by the Mandingo. Throughout the Soninke-Marabout Wars, the rulers of Wuli maintained a loose client relationship with Bakari Sardu, the ruler of Bondu, who used the territory as a corridor and staging ground for his raids into the Gambia. Despite a number of attempts, Musa Molloh of Fuladu was never able to add Wuli to his extensive kingdom. The rulers of Wuli cooperated fully with the various Boundary Commissions in the 1890s, and Yarbutenda, one of its river towns, became the terminal point for swinging the arcs defining the eastern boundary of the Gambia. Wuli was declared a District in the 20th century British reorganization of the Protectorate.

WYN HARRIS, SIR PERCY. Governor of the Gambia from 1949 to 1957. He supervised the minor extensions of political responsibility to allow Colony Gambians a larger voice in central government decisions. His period in office coincided with growing African nationalist sentiment in West Africa, and three political parties--the Muslim Congress, the Democratic Party, and the United Party--were formed in the Gambia to contest the elections for the Legislative Council in 1951 and 1954. His disagreements with P. J. N'Jie in 1955 resulted in the leader of the United Party refusing to serve any further in the liberalized government of the Colony area. Wyn Harris launched a modest program for the improvement of Protectorate agriculture. He was particularly interested in convincing Gambian farmers to increase rice production. Eventually the agricultural measures he favored helped to rid the Gambia of its "hungry season."

-Y-

YAMYAMAKUNDA. The site of one of the major Royal African Company factories along the Gambia River. It was located on the south bank approximately two miles northeast of the present village of Sankulekunda. The earlier factory was completely rebuilt by Francis Moore in the 1730s when he was a factor there.

YARBUTENDA. A town in the upper river district of Kantora. According to the Anglo-French Convention of 1889,

Yarbutenda was to be the key to defining the eastern
boundary of the Gambia.  The boundary was to be a
radius of 10 kilometers drawn with its center at Yarbutenda.  The survey commission of 1891 discovered
that the maps of the Gambia were incorrect since
there were two sites which could be considered the
town mentioned in the Convention.  Despite further
agreements between the French and British in 1898
and 1901, the eastern boundary was never satisfac-
torily determined on the ground.

YUNDUM.  A small town in Kombo which during the Soninke-
Marabout Wars was allied with the British.  Because
of this and because the chiefs of the town were Soninke,
it was an objective for Fodi Kabba, Fodi Silla, and
their followers.  In the late 1940s, it was the site of
the disasterous egg scheme sponsored by the British
Colonial Development Corporation.  Some of the
scheme's abandoned concrete buildings have been incorporated into the plant of the Gambia Teachers
Training College.  During World War II, the allies
situated an airfield at Yundum, and this has since become Gambia's international airport.

YUNDUM COLLEGE.  Prior to 1949, all Gambian teachers
received their training either in Sierra Leone or the
Gold Coast.  In that year a training center was opened
at Georgetown which offered a one-year course.  Most
of the buildings of the defunct egg scheme were acquired from the Colonial Development Corporation and
the Teachers Training College was moved to Yundum
in 1952.  In the following year, the course was opened
to women, and in 1954, the program was lengthened
to two years.  Beginning in 1955, major improvements
were made in the plant and the administration of the
college was separated from the Board of Education and
placed under a Board of Governors.

YUNDUM EGG SCHEME.  A plan put into effect by the
Colonial Development Corporation in the Fall of 1948
designed to make the Gambia a major exporter of eggs
and dressed chickens.  An initial appropriation of
£500,000 was made, and an American poultry expert,
Millard Phillips, was appointed field director.  The
plan was to clear the bush and timber and sell the
wood, and plant the prepared land in grain so that no
feed need be imported for the birds.  Permanent poultry

houses were built to accommodate enough chickens to
provide at maximum production 20 million eggs and
one million pounds of poultry per year.    The project
was plagued from the start by over optimistic estimates of the officials of the corporation and the field
staff who ignored the advice of Governor Wright and
his staff.    Timber from the cleared site was not of
export quality,  and the corporation had difficulty even
selling it for firewood.    By October 1950,  crop reports
showed an average grain yield of only 207 pounds per
acre as compared with estimates of 900 pounds per acre.
The poultry,  expensive Rhode Island Reds,  proved
highly susceptible to fowl pest and died by the thou-
sands.    By the time the Board of Directors of the Corporation agreed in February 1951 to close the project,
it had cost in direct appropriations £910,000.

# CHRONOLOGY OF IMPORTANT EVENTS

13th Century. Possible date of construction of stone circles by either Jola or Mandingo people. First southeastward migrations of significant numbers of Fulbe probably took place during this time.

13th to 15th Centuries. Period of Malian hegemony over the western Sudan. Gambian Mandingo kingdoms were the westernmost extension of that empire. Large numbers of Muslim converts appeared in the Senegambia.

16th to 17th Centuries. Period of state building among the Wolof in Senegal. Development of Jolof, Walo, Boal, and Cayor. Serer kingdoms of Sine and Saloum also developed in this period. First permanent European settlements in Senegambia during this time. Gradual acceleration of the slave trade.

18th Century. Creation of Islamic theocracy in the Futa Toro and continued conversion of large numbers of Gambians, particularly Fulbe, to Islam. Century-long French-British conflicts in Senegambia which disrupted trade and helped keep the slave trade to a minimal level.

1455 and 1456. First two Portuguese voyages (Cadamosto and Usidimare) to the Gambia River.

1458. Diego Gomez explored the Gambia River.

1553. First English voyages to the Gambia.

1588. First English monopoly company for West African trade.

1620. Richard Jobson, trade factor, sent to the Gambia.

1621. Dutch West Indies Company established at Goree.

1651. Courlanders in the Gambia; built fort on St. Andrews (James) Island. Commonwealth Guinea Company formed.

1652. Prince Rupert in the Gambia.

1660.   Royal Adventurers Company formed.

1661.   English captured James Island on March 19.

1668.   Gambia Adventurers Company established.

1672.   French Senegal Company formed.

1677.   French captured Goree.

1681.   French established Albreda.

1684-1750.   Royal African Company.

1689-1783.   Trade wars in Senegambia between France and Great Britain.

1696.   French Royal Senegal Company established.

1730.   Francis Moore, factor for Royal African Company, present in the Gambia.

1750.   Company of Merchants Trading in Africa formed.

1758.   French bases in Senegal captured.

1765-1783.   British Province of the Senegambia.

1779.   James Fort destroyed for last time.

1783-1820.   Gambia again controlled by Company of Merchants.

1790.   Major Houghton left the Gambia for Timbuktu.

1795-1798.   Mungo Park's explorations from the Gambia.

1805.   Beginning of Mungo Park's second expedition.

1808.   British abolition of the slave trade.

1816.   Purchase of St. Mary's Island from King of Kombo and beginnings of Bathurst (Banjul).

1821.   Gambia placed under jurisdiction of Sierra Leone.

1823.   First British establishment in April at MacCarthy Island.   Arrival of first contingent of Christian missionaries.

1826.   The King of Barra granted the Ceded Mile to Great Britain.

1827-1831.   The Barra War between the British and the King of Barra.

1830.   First recorded shipment of peanuts from the Gambia.

1843.   Gambia created a separate Colony with Executive and Legislative Councils.

1851. Beginnings of Soninke-Marabout Wars in Kombo.

1853. The King of Kombo ceded a portion of Kombo to the British.

1855. Marabout attack upon British Kombo and Bathurst.

1857. French surrender Albreda.

1860-1867. Ma Bâ attempted to create a Senegambia Islamic empire.

1861-1881. Alfa and Musa Molloh created the Fulbe state of Fuladu.

1862. Marabouts invade Barra.

1864. Amer Faal's operations in Niumi.  Fodi Kabba attacked Yundum.

1865. Report of Parliamentary Committee on West Africa.

1866. Gambia became a part of British West African Settlements once again.

1866-1870. First negotiations for exchange of the Gambia between Great Britain and France.

1873-1875. Fodi Silla destroys remaining Soninke power in Kombo.

1875-1876. Second period of negotiations for exchange of the Gambia between Great Britain and France.

1877-1887. Civil war in Baddibu between forces of Bairam Cisse, Saër Maty, and Mamadou N'Dare.

1888. Gambia became a separate colony; reinstatement of Legislative and Executive Councils.

1889. Anglo-French agreement which fixed the present boundaries of the Gambia.

1891. International Boundary Commission sent to Gambia.

1892. Fodi Kabba attacked Boundary Commission and was driven into the Casamance.

1894. Fodi Silla captured by the French and exiled.  First comprehensive Ordinance for governing the Protectorate.

1900. Travelling Commissioner Sitwell's party ambushed at Sankandi.

1901. British-French punitive expedition and death of Fodi Kabba.  Office of Administrator upgraded to Governor.

1904. Anglo-French Convention began the Entente and granted to the French the right for a mid-river port.

1913. General revision of Ordinance for the governing of the Protectorate.

1914-1918. First World War. Gambia Company of WAFF saw service in the Cameroon and East Africa.

1915. Enlargement of Legislative Council.

1919-1922. Redemption of French five franc piece.

1923. Opening of Armitage School, Georgetown.

1928. Bathurst Trade Union formed.

1931. Urban District Council created in Bathurst.

1932. Bathurst African nominated member appointed to Legislative Council.

1933. General reorganization of Protectorate government and courts system.

1935. Name of Urban District Council changed to Bathurst Town Council.

1939-1945. World War II. Gambian troops of WAFF active in China-Burma-India theater. Yundum airbase constructed for use by Allied ferry services.

1940. First British Colonial Development and Welfare Act.

1943. K. W. Blackburne's report on immediate and long-range economic needs of the Gambia.

1945-1950. Reconstruction of port, street, and sewer facilities of Bathurst (Banjul) with Colonial Development and Welfare funds.

1946. Reorganization and enlargement of Legislative Council.

1948-1951. Yundum egg fiasco.

1949-1952. Wallikunda rice scheme.

1951. New Constitution. Reorganization of Legislative Council which provided for two elected members from Bathurst. Democratic Party (DP) formed.

1952. Muslim Congress Party (MCP) formed. United Party (UP) formed. First class at Yundum College for teachers.

1953. Victoria Hospital opened in Bathurst (Banjul). Meeting of 34 Gambian representatives to revise Constitution.

1954. New Constitution allowing direct elective principle for seven members of the Legislative Council.

1957. Sinking of Barra ferry in May with loss of over 50 lives.

1959. Gambia Workers Union created. Protectorate People's Party formed; later called People's Progressive
Party (PPP).

1960. New Constitution; 34-member House of Representatives.
Democratic Congress Alliance (DCA) created.

1961. P. S. N'Jie became the first Gambian Chief Minister.

1962. New Constitution allowing full internal self government and a 36-member House of Representatives with
ministerial government. D. K. Jawara became Prime
Minister.

1963. First major comprehensive census of the Gambia.

1965. Voters reject proposal for a Republic. The Gambia
achieved independence from Great Britain on February 18.

1970. Voters approved proposals for a Republic in April.
Sir Dauda Jawara became the first President of the
Gambia.

## CONSTITUTIONAL ADVANCE SINCE 1938: A CHART

| Year | Legislature | | Elective Council or Ministry | |
|---|---|---|---|---|
| | Official Membership | Unofficial Membership | Official Membership | Unofficial Membership |
| 1938 | Governor + 6 | 4<br>(1 representing Muslim interests, 1 repr. commercial int., 2 repr. African int.) | Governor + 4 | None |
| 1947 | Governor + 3 ex-officio + 3 nominated | 7<br>(including 1 elected & 4 repr. Protect.) | Governor + 5 | 3<br>(2 nominated unofficials from Legislative Council and elected member) |
| 1952[a] | Governor + 3 ex-officio + 4 nominated | 8<br>(3 elected, 4 nominated to repr. the Divisions of Protectorate, 1 repr. commerce) | Governor + 6 | 4<br>(3 elected members of Legislative Council and 1 nominated, of whom 2 were appointed members of the Government without Portfolio) |
| 1954[b] | Governor + 4 ex-officoi (incl. Senior Commissioner + 1 Gambian Public Officer | 16<br>4 directly elected by Colony<br>7 directly elected by Protec.<br>3 elected by these 11<br>1 nominated to rep. commerce<br>1 other nominated | Governor + 5 (as for Leg. Council) | 7<br>(of whom 3 have been appointed Ministers) |
| 1960[c] | 4 ex-officio 3 nominated | 27<br>(7 directly elected by Colony<br>12 directly elected by Protect.<br>8 chosen by Protect. chiefs) | Governor + 4 | 6<br>(4 Ministers directly responsible for government departments) |
| 1962 | | 36<br>(7 directly elected by Colony<br>25 directly elected by Protect.<br>4 chosen by Protect. chiefs) | Governor + 4 | 8 Ministers<br>of a Responsible Government under direction of Chief Minister |

[a]Vice President appointed;   [b]Speaker to be appointed by the Governor;   [c]Name of Legislature changed to House of Representatives

## CHIEF EXECUTIVES, 1829-(1974)

### Governors and Administrators

| | | |
|---|---|---|
| 1829 | Lieutenant-Colonel Alexander Findlay | Lieut. Governor |
| 1830 | George Rendall | " " |
| 1840 | Sir Henry Huntley | " " |
| 1843 | Captain H. F. Seagram, R.N. | Governor |
| 1843 | E. Norcott | " |
| 1844 | Commander G. Fitzgerald, R.N. | " |
| 1847 | Sir R. G. MacDonnell | " |
| 1852 | A. E. Kennedy | " |
| 1852 | Colonel L. S. O'Connor | " |
| 1859 | Colonel G. A. K. D'Arcy | " |
| 1866 | Admiral C. G. E. Patey, C.M.C. | Administrator |
| 1871 | T. F. Callaghan, C.M.G. | " |
| 1873 | Sir C. H. Kortright, C.M.G. | " |
| 1875 | Sir Samuel Rowe, K.C.M.G. | " |
| 1877 | Dr. V. S. Gouldsbury, C.M.G. | " |
| 1884 | Sir C. A. Moloney, K.C.M.G. | " |
| 1886 | Sir J. S. Hay, K.C.M.G. | " |
| 1888 | Sir Gilbert T. Carter, K.C.M.G. | " |
| 1891 | Sir R. B. Llewellyn, K.C.M.G. | " |
| 1901 | Sir G. C. Denton, K.C.M.G. | Governor |
| 1911 | Lieutenant-Colonel Sir H. L. Galway, K.C.M.G., D.S.O. | " |
| 1914 | Sir Edward J. Cameron, K.C.M.G. | " |
| 1920 | Captain Sir C. H. Armitage, K.B.E., C.M.G., D.S.O. | " |
| 1927 | Sir John Middleton, K.B.E., C.M.G. | " |
| 1928 | Sir Edward Denham, K.C.M.G., K.B.E. | " |
| 1930 | Sir H. Richmond Palmer, K.C.M.G., C.B.E. | " |
| 1933 | Sir Arthur Richards, K.C.M.G. | " |
| 1936 | Sir Wilfred T. Southorn, K.C.M.G., K.B.E. | " |
| 1942 | Sir Hilary Blood, K.C.M.G. | " |
| 1947 | Sir Andrew B. Wright, K.C.M.G. | " |
| 1949 | Sir P. Wyn Harris, K.C.M.G., M.B.E. | " |
| 1957 | Sir Edward Windley, K.C.M.G., C.B.E. | " |
| 1962 | Sir John Paul, M.C. | " |
| 1966 | Alhaji Farimang Singhateh | " |

### Gambian Chief Executives

| | | |
|---|---|---|
| 1961 | Pierre S. N'Jie, United Party | Chief Minister |
| 1962 | Sir Dauda Jawara, People's Prog. Party | Prime Minister |
| 1970 | "        "         "          "         "        " | President |

141

BIBLIOGRAPHY

    Although there is a considerable body of literature
related to the Gambia, the bulk of this material exists as
specialized government reports or traveller's accounts.
There have been only a few authors who focused upon the
Gambia during the explosive period of research and writing
on African territories following World War II.  Thus this
crucial epoch of political and social ferment has been ne-
glected, and persons concerned with the Gambia are forced
to turn to a very fragmented list of books and articles in
order to gain some insight into the modern period.   To
assist the reader in determining the most relevant works,
the following bibliography has been selectively annotated.
Note that under some "ARTICLES" and "(Government Papers)"
sections, in the absence of many author entries, arrangement is chronological.

    In order to facilitate the task of finding material on
specific subjects, the works have been classified according
to the following scheme:

GENERAL
  Exploration/Travel
    Books
      15th-16th Centuries
      17th Century
      18th Century
      19th Century
      20th Century
    Articles
  Guides
    Pamphlets
    Articles

CULTURAL
  Literature
  Linguistic
  Press

ECONOMIC
  Agriculture
    Books
      Gambia Gov. Reports
      G. B. Colonial Off. Rpts.
    Development
      Gambia Gov. Reports
      G. B. Papers
      Articles
    Finance
      Gambia Gov. Reports
      Misc. Reports
    Labor
      Gambia Gov. Reports
      Articles
    Transport
      Gambia Gov. Reports

142

HISTORICAL
  15th-19th Centuries
    Books
    Articles
    G. B. Colonial Off. Papers
  20th Century
    Books
    Articles

POLITICAL
  Constitution
    Gambia Gov. Papers
    G. B. Papers
    Articles
  Government
    Books
    Gambia Gov. Papers
    Articles
    Gambia Gov. Ordinances
  Law
  Political Parties
  Foreign Affairs

G. B. Papers
  Articles

SCIENTIFIC
  Geography
    Books
    Articles
  Geology
  Medicine
  Natural Science

SOCIAL
  Anthropology/Archaeology
    Books
    Articles
  Demography
    Gambia Gov. Reports
  Education
    Gambia Gov. Reports
  Religion
  Sociology

GENERAL:   Exploration and Travel

## BOOKS

15th and 16th Centuries:

Asseline, David.  Les Antiquités et chroniques de la ville de
    Dieppe, 2 vols. (Dieppe: 1874).

Hakluyt, Richard.  Principal Navigations of the English Na-
    tion, 5 vols. (London: 1927).  See particularly Vol. IV,
    pp. 285 & Vol. V, pp. 44-52.

Hakluyt Society.  The Voyages of Cadamosto and other Docu-
    ments on Western Africa in the Second Half of the 15th
    Century (London: 1937).  Cadamosto, the discover of the
    Gambia River for Prince Henry in the journals of his two
    voyages of the mid-15th century, gives the first reliable
    European account of the river and its inhabitants.

Monod, Theodore, ed.  Description de la Côte Occidentale
    d'Afrique par Valentin Fernandes (1506-1510) (Paris:
    1938), pp. 25-27.  One of the earliest European accounts
    of the tribal dispositions near the coastline of Senegambia.

17th Century:

Barbot, Jean. Description of the Coasts of North and South Guinea (London: 1732). The first edition of this work was prepared some time in the 1680s. See particularly p. 70 ff.

Cultru, Prosper. Premier Voyage de Sieur de la Courbe (Paris: 1918).

Jobson, Richard. The Golden Trade (London: 1932). Jobson was sent out as supercargo on a trading expedition by the Royal Adventurers of England in 1620 to relieve a previous expedition and to carry on trade with the natives on the river. He and others proceeded upriver as far as Barrakunda Falls. Although their trading exports did not result in a profit for the company, Jobson's notes and comments form a classic of African travel.

Le Maire, M. Voyage to the Canaries, Cape Verd and the Coast of Africa under the Command of M. Dancourt, 1682 (Edinburgh: 1887). See particularly pp. 35-60. An excellent description is given of the remains of the Portuguese influence in the river on p. 47. The first publication of this work was in Paris in 1695.

Perrot, Nicolas. L'Afrique de Marmol--de la traduction de Nicolas Perrot, 3 vols. (Paris: 1667). See Vol. III, pp. 70-90.

Rochefort, Jannequin de. Voyage de Libye au Royaume Genega (Paris: 1643).

Stibbs, Capt. B. Journal of a Voyage up the Gambia (London: 1732). Stibbs was the sub-commander of James Island who undertook an exploratory voyage to the upper Gambia in 1724. This Journal relates his experiences and observations. His reports of native stories of vast riches in the further interior helped to create the myth of the myth of the secret gold mines that motivated many 18th-century traders. The Journal is also reproduced in Francis Moore's Travels.

Thevenot, Melchisedech. Memoires du voyage aux Indes Orientales du Général Beaulieu (Paris: 1672). Contains a description of the first attempt by the French to settle a colony and build a fort on the Gambia River in 1612.

Warburton, Eliot.  Memoirs of Prince Rupert and the Cava-
liers, 3 vols.  (London: 1849).  Vol. 3 is the most pertinent for the Gambia since it contains the record of
Prince Rupert's activities on the Gambia River directed
against the Commonwealth including the sacking of Bintang.  Rupert also reported tales of a mountain of pure
gold located somewhere in the upper river area.

18th Century:

Adanson, M.  A Voyage to Senegal, the Isle of Goree and
the River Gambia (London: 1759).  Observations made
by a French naturalist who visited the Senegambia in
1749.  See particularly pp. 156-172 for description of
coastal tribes.

Astley, Thomas.  A New General Collection of Voyages and
Travels, 4 vols.  (London: 1745).  Vols. 1 and 2 contain
many of the older travel accounts--Cadamosto, Barbot,
de Rochefort, Le Maire, and others.  As such, because
the originals are hard to obtain, it is one of the most
valuable composite works dealing with West Africa.

Blagdon, Francis.  Modern Discoveries (London: 1802).
Vols. 3 and 4 contain S. M. X. Golbery, "Fragments
d'un voyage en Afrique (1785-1787)."  The most important
section of Blagdon's work is the translation of Golbery's
observations made between the years 1785-87.  Golbery
served the French in the Senegambia for a number of
years, and his work is particularly useful for details of
French trading ventures there.

Churchill, John.  A Collection of Voyages (London: 1744).
Contains older accounts such as Courbe and Barbot.

Golbery, Silvanius Meinrad Xavier.  Fragments d'un voyage
en Afrique (1785-1787), 2 vols.  (Paris: 1802).

Labat, Jean Baptiste.  Nouvelle relation de l'Afrique Occidentale, 5 vols. (Paris: 1728).  Particularly Vol. 1, pp.
304-307; Vol. 4, pp. 256-264, 367-380; Vol. 5, pp. 2-
22, 307-324.  This is an account of the travels and
policies of Andre Brue who was sent out in 1697 to
Goree to be Director General of the French Senegal
Company.  See particularly Vol. 1, pp. 304-307 and
Vol. 5, pp. 2-22 and 307-324 for tribal alignments and
customs in the Gambia.

Moore, Francis.  Travels in the Inland Part of Africa (London: 1738).  Moore was a scholarly young man sent by the Royal African Company to be a "writer" at James Island in 1730.  He survived four years and left behind a monumental work of observation concerning peoples, customs, trade, insects, and animals which also contains very lucid insights into social and political organizations.  This work read in conjunction with Jobson also shows how much had changed in the Gambia in the course of a century.  Also appended to Moore's notes is Stibbs, Journal of an earlier exploratory voyage.

Park, Mungo.  Travels in the Interior Districts of Africa (London: 1899).  The Travels are concerned with the Gambia only to the extent that Park used the Gambia as his point of departure and he did describe the people of the Gambia very vividly.  He left Pisania (Karantaba) in December 1795 after a six-month stay at the home of Dr. Laidley.  His observations of local customs and color are matched only by Francis Moore's writings.

Smith, William.  A New Voyage to Guinea (London: 1744).  See p. 32 ff. for a description of Smith's visit to the Gambia in 1726-27.

Walckenaer, Charles Athanase.  Collections des relations de voyages par mer et par terre en différentes parties de l'Afrique, 2 vols. (Paris: 1842).

19th Century:

Alexander, James E.  Narrative of a Voyage of Observation Among the Colonies of West Africa, 2 vols. (London: 1853).  A good account of Bathurst and prospects of tapping interior trade from there is given in Vol. 1, pp. 70-72.

Biller, Sarah.  Memoir of Hannah Kilham (London: 1837).  Mrs. Kilham, a member of the Society of Friends, was one of the earliest missionaries to the Gambia.  She began studying Wolof and preparing school books before going to the Gambia in 1823.

Bowdich, T. E.  Excursions in Maderia and Porto Santa, to which is added ... "A description of the English Settlements on the River Gambia" by Mrs. Bowdich, (London: 1825).  Mrs. Bowdich's account of the Gambia begins on p. 204.

[Burton, Richard F.] "An F.R.G.S." Wanderings in West
     Africa, 2 vols. (London: 1863). The famous explorer
     and Islamic scholar spent a few days in the vicinity of
     Bathurst and left a rather negative traveller's version
     of the worthlessness of the Gambia.

Ellis, A. B. The Land of Fetish (London: 1883). A very
     superficial account by an officer who was stationed in
     the Gambia for a brief time. For his impressions of
     the Gambia see pp. 1-34.

Gaunt, Mary. Alone in West Africa (London: 1912). Chapter
     2 contains her impressions of the Gambia.

Gray, Major William. Travels in Western Africa in the
     Years 1819-1821 from the River Gambia, thru Woolli,
     Bondoo, Galam, Kassan, Kaarta and Foolidoo to the
     River Niger (London: 1825). See particularly p. 46 ff.
     and pp. 192-194.

Hewitt, J. F. Napier. European Settlements on the West
     Coast of Africa (London: 1862). Hewitt was a more than
     usually prejudiced observer of the British administration
     of the Gambia. Provides a counterbalance to the more
     favorable reports by other 19th-century travellers.

Huntley, Sir Henry. Seven Years' Service on the Slave Coast
     of Western Africa, 2 vols. (London: 1850). Huntley was
     the third Lieutenant-Governor of the Gambia, assuming
     his post in 1840. Considering the important administra-
     tive problems of the Gambia at that time, this work is
     remarkably noninformative. Primarily useful as a
     traveller's account.

Mitchinson, A. W. The Expiring Continent, A Narrative of
     Travel in the Senegambia, etc. (London: 1881). A travel
     book.

Mollien, G. Travels in the Interior of Africa to the Sources
     of the Senegal and Gambia in the Year 1818, ed. T. E.
     Bowdich, (London: 1820). The work deals primarily with
     Mollien's explorations and is of slight value for the Gam-
     bia except in the reports of the customs of people of the
     same tribe as those who lived in the Gambia Valley.

Morgan, John. Reminiscences of the Founding of a Christian
     Mission on the Gambia (London: 1864). Contains some

brief glimpses into the life and customs of the Wolof and Mandingo people.

Park, Mungo. Journal of a Mission to the Interior of Africa in the Year 1805 (London: 1815). On his ill-fated second journey in 1805, Park also left from Pisania, and it was to this place that his interpreter, Issaco, brought the Journal. The Journal, although a necessary supplement to the earlier Travels, has even less to say about the Gambia.

Poole, T. E. Life, Scenery & Customs in Sierra Leone and the Gambia, 2 vols. (London: 1850). Poole was Colonial and Garrison Chaplain of Sierra Leone from 1845-50. His impressions of the Gambia are in Vol. 2, pp. 70-85; 138-140, and 205 ff.

Rançon, A. Dans la Haute-Gambie. Voyage d'exploration scientifique, 1891-1892 (Paris: 1894). Valuable only as a corrollary account of areas adjacent to the Gambia.

Reade, W. Winwood. Savage Africa (London: 1864). A naive and superficial account of the Senegambia is in Chapters 30-33.

Whitford, John. Trading Life in Western and Central Africa (London: 1877). See pp. 18-22 for the Gambia.

Wilson, J. L. Western Africa, Its History Conditions and Prospects (London: 1856).

Wood, J. Dobson. To West Africa and Back (London: 1894). A general travel account of a trip to Gambia and the Canary Islands.

20th Century:

Crowder, Michael. Pagans and Politicians (London: 1959). The book was a result of a journey made by the author immediately after his university training--not a typical European voyage, but one on the cheap. Crowder met the people on their own level. Pp. 25-43 represents his impression of the Gambia.

Gunther, John. Inside Africa (New York: 1955). Little inside information is to be found on pp. 742-745.

Hardinge, R.  Gambia and Beyond (London: 1934).  A brief superficial travel account.

Hempstone, Smith.  Africa, Angry Young Giant (New York: 1961).  Pp. 359-392 deals with the Gambia.  Hempstone is not just a casual traveller, and in one brief chapter he shows considerable insight into the society and modern problems of the Gambia.

Rice, Berkeley.  Enter Gambia, The Birth of an Improbable Nation (Boston: 1967).  Rice's improbable book, despite its lack of organization, is quite valuable in recording his impressions of the Gambian scene during the period immediately after independence.

Willis, Colin.  White Traveller in Black Africa (London: 1951).  The author is a most intelligent, journalistic observer of the African scene.  Chapter 10 concerns the Gambia.

## ARTICLES

Hadson, H.  "Golden Gambia," Travel, Jan. 1957, pp. 52-54.

MacColl, R.  "Gambia, The Colony Nobody Knows," Atlantic, May 1962, pp. 108-112.

Phillips, R. H.  "Up River through the Gambia," Crown Colonist, 1933, pp. 249-50.

Porter, Sibyl.  "Gambia Journey," West African Review, April 1952, pp. 330-32.  Story of a ten-day trek through the Gambia Protectorate.

Rice, B.  "Enter Gambia, Laughing," Harpers, Oct. 1966, pp. 74-78.

Van der Plas, C. O.  "Discovering the Gambia," United Nations Review, Dec. 1958, pp. 15-19.

GENERAL:  Guides

## PAMPHLETS

The Gambia (London, 1967).

The Gambia ... in Brief (Portsmouth, 1967).  Both of these

were issued by the Gambian Government as aids for tourists.

## ARTICLES

Gailey, Harry A. "African Archives--Gambia," Africana Newsletter, Vol. I, no. 3, 1963.

_____. "Bibliographic Essays--The Gambia," Africana Newsletter, Vol. II, no. 1, 1964.

## CULTURAL: Literature

There have been few literary works whose locale was the Gambia, and the two most successful authors born in the territory have chosen to write in generalized African terms. The action in William Conton's The African takes place in an area obviously not the Gambia. Lenrie Peters, one of the finest modern poets, addresses his audience in more universal terms. The only novels which refer specifically to the Gambia are: John Bingley, Mr. Khoury (London: 1952) and Margery Lawrence, The Gilded Jar (London: 1948).

## CULTURAL: Linguistics

Faye, J. C., and M. A. Sillah. The Orthography of Gambian Languages--Wolof and Mandinka (Bathurst: 1956).

Gamble, D. P. Mandinka Reading Book (Bathurst: 1956).

_____. Notes on Mandinka (Bathurst: 1949).

Hopkinson, Emilius. Mandingo Vocabulary (1911; with addenda 1924).

MacBrian, the Rev. R. M. A Grammar of the Mandingo Language with Vocabularies (London: 1937).

Nunn, G. N. N. A Short Phrase Book and Classified Vocabulary from English into Mandinka (Bathurst: 1934).

O'Halloran, G., and F. Sidible. Mandinka Talibe la Kitabo (Bathurst: 1948).

Rowlands, E. C. A Grammar of Gambian Mandinka (London: 1959).

CULTURAL:  Press

Gambia Echo, weekly.

Gambia News Bulletin, published three times a week by the
Gambia Government Information Service.

Kibaro.  Issued monthly in late 1940s by the Senior Commissioner, Marina, Bathurst.  Written in Mandinka language
in Roman script.

The Nation, monthly.

News Gambia, weekly.


ECONOMIC:  Agriculture

## BOOKS

Dawe, M. T.  Report on the Agricultural Conditions and
Needs of the Gambia (Bathurst: 1921).

Dudgeon, G. G.  The Agricultural and Forest Products of
British West Africa (London: 1911).  For the Gambia
see pp. 1-14.

Moloney, A.  Sketch of the Forestry of West Africa (London:
1887).

## GAMBIA GOVERNMENT REPORTS

Brooks, A. J.  "The Cultivation of Groundnuts," Department
of Agriculture Bulletin #3 (1929).

Palmer, J. H.  "Notes on Strange Farmers," Sessional
Paper #15 (1946).

Pirie, J.  "Vegetable Cultivation.  Hints to Protectorate
Farmers," Department of Agriculture Bulletin #3 (1929).

Rodden, G. M.  "A Report of Rice Cultivation in the Gambia," Sessional Paper #2 (1943).

Roe, C. J.  "Report on Swamp Reclamation and the Improvement of Existing Rice Lands by Drainage, Irrigation, etc.,
in the Gambia," Sessional Paper #1 (1943).

Rosevear, D. R.  "Report on the Forest Conditions of the
    Gambia" (1936).

Van der Plas, C. O.  "Report of a Survey of Rice Areas in
    the Central Division of the Gambia Protectorate" (August
    1955).

_____.  "A Summary of the Conclusions and Recommenda-
    tions of the Conference on Cooperative Societies held at
    University College, Ibadan, 13-17 December 1954" (1955).

Agriculture Department Report.  Annual, from 1924.

Forestry Department Annual Report.  From 1950.  Issued as
    Sessional Papers of the Legislative Council.

Gambia Oilseeds Marketing Board.  Annual Report.  From
    1949-50.

Gambian Rice Farm.  Annual Report.

        GREAT BRITAIN, COLONIAL OFFICE REPORTS

Haswell, M. R.  Economics of Agriculture in a Savannah
    Village, 1953.

_____.  The Changing Pattern of Economic Activity in a
    Gambian Village, 1963.

ECONOMIC:  Development

        GAMBIA GOVERNMENT REPORTS

Blackburne, K. W., et al.  "Development and Welfare in
    the Gambia" (1943).

"Report of a Committee Appointed to Consider Remedial
    Measures to be Adopted to Deal with Over-crowding in
    Bathurst" (1946).

"Correspondence with the Secretary of State for the Colonies
    on the Replanning of Bathurst and the Development of
    Kombo," Sessional Paper #1 (1944).

"Secretary of State's Reply to the Second Application for
    Assistance under C. D. W. Act for Bathurst/Kombo,"
    Sessional Paper #12 (1945).

"Exploration for Petroleum Deposits in Gambia," Sessional
    Paper #6 (1959).

"Gambian Government, Development Plan, 1964-67," Sessional
    Paper #10 (1964).

"Revision of the Development Programme 1964-67," Sessional
    Paper #1 (1966).

"Gambia Government, 1967-68 to 1970-71," Sessional Paper
    #4 (1967).

### GREAT BRITAIN, PAPERS BY COMMAND

"Statement of Policy on Colonial Development and Welfare,"
    Cmd. 6175 (Feb. 1940).

"Report on the Gambian Egg Scheme," Cmd. 8560.

### ARTICLES

Crowder, M.   "Chicken Coop' College--Aftermath of the
    Gambia Egg Farm," West African Review, 1956.

Ivor, Thomas.   "Lessons of Gambia Poultry Farm," New
    Commonwealth, August 1951, pp. 88-89.

"Rehousing and Townplanning in the Gambia," West African
    Review, Oct. 1946, pp. 1123-24.

"Bathurst Drainage and Reclamation Work," New Common-
    wealth, 1947, pp. 605-606.

"Gambia Chicken Farm," West African Review, Dec. 1948,
    p. 1423.

"Gambia's Georgia Man--M. J. Phillips," CDC., West
    Africa, 3 June 1950, p. 485.

"CDC Statement on the Gambian Egg Scheme," West Africa,
    21 April 1951, p. 357.

"Lord Trefgarne on the Gambia Poultry Scheme," West
    Africa, 21 April 1951, p. 351.

ECONOMIC:    Finance

## GAMBIA GOVERNMENT REPORTS

"Report of Commission to Investigate and Report on the Financial Position of the Colony" (1953).

"Statement of Government Policy Regarding Groundnut Prices
and the Use of a Stabilization Fund and Kindred Matters,
1955" (1955).

"The Financial Position--Exchange of Despatches Between the
Government and Secretary of State for the Colonies, "
Sessional Paper #11 (1960).

Loynes, J. B.    "Report on the Problem of the Future Cur-
rencies of Sierra Leone and the Gambia, " Sessional
Paper #12 (1961).

"Account General, Financial Report with Appendices, 1964, "
Sessional Paper #9 (1966).

"Address of the Governor-General at the Budget Session of
the House of Representatives, 22 June 1967, " Sessional
Paper #5 (1967).

"British Financial Aid to the Gambia, 1967/68 to 1970/71, "
Sessional Paper #7 (1967).

## MISCELLANEOUS REPORTS

Great Britain, Cmd. 1600.    "Report of a Committee on Trade
and Taxation for British West Africa" (1922).

International Labour Organisation.    "Expanded Programme of
Technical Assistance-Report to Government of the Gambia
on Cooperative Banking" (1964).

_____.    "Expanded Programme of Technical Assistance-
Second Report to Government of the Gambia on Cooperative Banking" (1965).

United States. Bureau of Foreign Commerce.    "Import Tariff
System of Gambia" (World Trade Information Service
Operation Report (61-33), (April 1961).

ECONOMIC: Labor

## GAMBIA GOVERNMENT REPORTS

"Commission to Investigate the Basic Terms and Conditions of Daily rated Labour, " Sessional Paper #2 (1959).

## ARTICLES

Gailey, Harry A. "Fixing the Rate for Gambia Jobs, " West Africa, Feb. 11, 1961, p. 151.

_____. "Portrait, Gambia's Labour Leader, " West Africa, May 17, 1961, p. 569.

_____. "Jallow's Progress, " Portrait, West Africa, May 2, 1964, p. 481.

"New Act on Wages in Gambia, " International Labour Review, Oct. 1966, p. 416.

ECONOMIC: Transport

## GAMBIA GOVERNMENT REPORTS

"Report of a Committee Appointed to Enquire into the Conduct and Management of the River Steamer Service, " Sessional Paper #11 (1944).

"Report of the Committee Appointed to Consider Remedial Measures to be Adopted to Deal with Overcrowding in Bathurst, " Sessional Paper #18 (1946).

HISTORICAL: 15th-19th Centuries

## BOOKS

Archer, F. Bisset. The Gambia Colony and Protectorate (London: 1906). The author was a former civil servant in the Gambia and the book's strengths and weaknesses reflect his primary vocation. It is a mine of factual information concerning British activities in the Gambia in the 19th century.

Blake, J. W. European Beginnings in West Africa (London: 1937). This work, in combination with those of Davies and Martin, serves as an excellent introduction to the early history of Europeans in western Africa.

Cultru, Prosper.  Histoire du Sénégal (Paris: 1910).  An older work that still remains in many ways the best history of Senegal.

Davies, K. G.  The Royal African Company (London: 1957). The Royal African Company played the most important role in the British trading spheres in West Africa for almost a century.  Davies' work is invaluable in evaluating the nature and scope of British activities.  The Senegambia was considered a minor arena for their trading operations.  Most of the book is devoted to the more economically viable areas.  Nevertheless, anyone dealing with the Senegambia must consult at least the pertinent sections of this book.

Deschamps, Hubert.  Le Sénégal et la Gambie (Paris: 1964).

Diederich, Heinrich.  Herzog Jakobs von Kurland Kolonien an der Westkuste von Afrika (Miltau: 1890).  This book is still useful for a background to the Courlander experiment, although it has largely been supplanted by Mattiesen.

Eckert, Walter.  Kurland unter dem Einfluss des Merkantilismus, 1551-1682 (Riga: 1927).  Contains an excellent if somewhat dated account of the Courlander's colonizing efforts in the 17th century.

Fitzgerald, H. E.  The Gambia and Its Proposed Cession to France (London: 1875).  A brief panegyric on the question of exchanging the Gambia.

Gray, Sir John M.  A History of the Gambia (Cambridge: 1940; reprinted London: 1966).  Gray was a former Justice in the Gambian Supreme Court and, as his later works on East Africa attest, an accomplished scholar. This history is probably the best single volume work ever published on the Gambia.  Sir John utilized archival materials both in England and the Gambia.  The work is particularly useful in detailing the early trade rivalries of the European powers and for the intricate patterns of African conflicts in the 19th century.  It is, however, not an interpretive work and further, it is not concerned with the 20th century developments in the Senegambia.

Hamlyn, W. T.   A Short History of the Gambia (Bathurst: 1931).  This is a very short non-detailed secondary school textbook which was brought up to date through World War II by Hamlyn with the publication of Stories of the Gambia (Bathurst: 1945).

Klein, Martin.  Islam and Imperialism in Senegal (Stanford: 1968).  The sections pp. 63-113 give the best detailed description of Ma Bâ and the Soninke-Marabout conflict.

Lawrence, A. W.   Trade Castles and Forts of West Africa (London: 1963).  Contains good descriptions of the building of early European forts in the Senegambia. See particularly pp. 250-261 for James Fort.

Martin, Evelyne.  The British West Africa Settlements 1750-1821 (London: 1927).  Martin's work is complementary to that of Davies.  The years involved in this study cover the transition period from rule by the Royal African Company to the assumption of direct control by the Crown.

Mattiesen, Otto Heinz.  Die Kolonial und Überseepolitik der kurlandischen Herzöge im 17 und 18 Jahrhundert (Stuttgart: 1940).  This is one of the most difficult works to obtain which treat of European colonization in the 17th century.  It is the finest work on the subject of Courland's short-lived colonial experiments in Africa and the West Indies.  The long scholarly discussion on their efforts in the Senegambia is particularly well done.

Palmer, H. R.   The Carthaginian Voyage to West Africa (Bathurst: 1931).  Palmer was a governor of the Gambia who had served many years in Nigeria.  He was a very good amateur historian and linguist.  The first portion of this book deals with the probability that Hanno, the Carthaginian sailor, reached the Senegambia.

Pfeffer, Karl Heinz.  Sierra Leone and Gambia (Bonn: 1958). This is a short generalized work on the two British African territories.

Quinn, Charlotte.  "Mandingo States in Nineteenth Century Gambia" in Carleton T. Hodge, ed., Papers on Manding (Bloomington, Ind.: 1971).  This is the best detailed coverage of the organization, development and conflict of Gambian Mandingo states during this crucial period.

Reeve, Henry F.  The Gambia (London: 1912).  Reeve was
    another civil servant in the Gambia.  His book is well
    written and is not only a political history, but contains
    a description of peoples, languages, customs, and the
    flora and fauna of the area.  Notwithstanding the un-
    developed state of anthropological knowledge at that time,
    Reeve shows some excellent insights.  Read together
    with Gray's History, it becomes an invaluable secondary
    work.

Sabatie, A.  Le Sénégal, sa conquête et son organisation,
    1364-1925 (Paris: 1962).  One of the better organized
    accounts of French activity in the Senegambia.  It con-
    tains much useful material on all periods of French
    interest in the Gambia.  It is a particularly good pre-
    sentation of the French point of view in the crucial years
    1880-1900.

Verdier, A.  Exchange de Territoire Coloniale (La Rochelle:
    1876).  A pamphlet opposing the exchange of territory
    in West Africa with Britain.

Young, Frederick, et al.  Report of the Council of the Royal
    Colonial Institute on the Gambia Question (London: 1876).
    Issued to convince the government that the Gambia was
    valuable and should not be traded.

ARTICLES

Currey, E. Hamilton.  "Boat Actions and River Fights--The
    Baddiboo War," United Service Magazine, Vol. 49, 1914,
    pp. 124-133.

Gray, John.  "Zimmerman's 18th Century Gambia Journey,"
    African Affairs, Feb. 1959, pp. 65-74.

Harden, D. B.  "The Phoenicians on the West Coast of
    Africa," Antiquity, Sept. 1948, pp. 141-150.

Macklin, B. W.  "Queens and Kings of Niumi," Man, May
    1935.

Mahoney, Florence K.  "African Leadership in Bathurst in
    the Nineteenth Century," Tarikh, Vol. 2, No. 2, 1968.

Quinn, Charlotte.  "Maba Diakhou Bâ, Scholor-Warrior of
    the Senegambia," Tarikh, Vol. 2, No. 3, 1968.

_____. "A Nineteenth Century Fulbe State," Journal
African History, Vol. 12, No. 3, 1971, pp. 427-440.

Southorn, Lady Bella. "James Island," West African Review, May 1949, pp. 484-489, pp. 506-507 (photographs).

Southorn, Sir Wilfred Thomas. "Earliest British Settlement in Africa," Crown Colonist, 1943, pp. 391-392.

Wood, W. Raymond. "An Archaeological Appraisal of Early
European Settlements in the Senegambia," The Journal
of African History, Vol. 8, No. 1, 1967, pp. 39-64.

GREAT BRITAIN, COLONIAL OFFICE PAPERS

"A Reply of the Merchants of the Gambia to the Despatches
of Sir Arthur Kennedy," West African Pamphlet #1
(1870).

"Correspondence Relating to the Territories on the River
Gambia," African #348 (1887).

"Correspondence Relating to British and French Jurisdiction,"
African #377 (1890).

"Correspondence Relating to the Gambian Expedition" (1901).
The details of the joint French-English expedition against
Fodi Kabba and Musa Molloh.

HISTORICAL:    20th Century

BOOKS

Gailey, Harry A.  A History of the Gambia (London: 1964).
Although the history of the Gambia before 1900 is sum-
marized, the main emphasis of this work is upon 20th-
century developments to the eve of independence.  It is
the only detailed treatment of the Gambia in the 20th
century.

Great Britain. Foreign Office. Historical Section.  Peace
Handbooks (London: 1920).  Vol. 15, No. 91 contains a
brief survey of the Gambia; Vol. 17, No. 102 reports in
a simple fashion concerning the Senegal.

Huxley, Elspeth.  Four Guineas (London: 1954).  Chapter 1
is devoted to the Gambia.  This is certainly one of the

y this very gifted observer of Africa. She
ew days in the Gambia and this combined
African background enabled her to draw a
of wrong conclusions.

Gambia (Bonn: 1965). This is a very
pamphlet.

Southorn, ~~Lady~~ ella. The Gambia (London: 1952). A very
interesting book written by the wife of a former governor.
Lady Southorn's book depends largely upon personal observation and the factual underpinning of Reeve and Gray.
It is a combination history and eyewitness account which
because of her skill renders the people and customs
more alive than any work on the Gambia written in the
20th century.

Welch, Claude. Dream of Unity (Ithaca, N. Y.: 1966). The
section pp. 250-292 contains an excellent discussion of
the background to an early development of the movement
for a united Senegambia.

## ARTICLES

Armitage, Capt. C. H. "The Gambia Colony and Protectorate," Journal of the Royal Society of Arts, 22 June
1928, pp. 811-818.

Langley, M. "Gambia: Trading Post to Independent Nation,"
History Today, June 1965, pp. 420-425.

POLITICAL: Constitution

GAMBIA GOVERNMENT, SPECIALIZED PUBLICATIONS

Consultative Committee on the Constitution. "Report. 1953,"
Gazette, Vol. 70, July 31, 1953.

"An Act to Establish and Make Provisions for the Constitution of the Gambia," The Gazette (Supplement), No. 4,
Nov. 1969.

"Proposed Constitutional Changes in the Gambia," Sessional
Paper #27 (1953).

"Constitutional Development in the Gambia," Sessional Paper
#4 (1959).

"Constitutional Development in the Gambia," Sessional Paper #6 (1961).

GREAT BRITAIN, SPECIALIZED PUBLICATIONS

Central Office of Information. Constitutional Progress in the Gambia, 1955.

Cmnd. 1468. "Report of Gambian Constitutional Conference" (1961).

Cmnd. 2435. "The Gambia Independence Conference" (1964).

ARTICLES

Gailey, Harry A. "What Next in the Gambia," West Africa, Part I, 22 July 1961, p. 801; Part II, 29 July 1961, p. 861.

"Gambia and Malta," West Africa, 11 Jan. 1958, p. 25.

"Independence Aim," New Commonwealth, Dec. 1960, p. 809.

Land, Harry. "What Status for Sierra Leone and Gambia," New Commonwealth, Sept. 1960, pp. 568-570.

"Universal Suffrage for the Gambia," New Commonwealth, Oct. 1959, pp. 683-684.

POLITICAL:   Government

BOOKS

Hailey, (Lord). Native Administration in the British African Territories, 4 vols. (London: 1950). Vol. III, pp. 329-350 treats in great detail the instruments of the Gambia government through 1951.

Hertslet, Sir Edward. Map of Africa by Treaty (London: 1894). An invaluable work, particularly for the historian of late 19th-century Africa. Hertslet has reproduced the major treaties between the great powers and also those between the European states and major native rulers.

GAMBIA GOVERNMENT, SPECIALIZED PUBLICATIONS

"Instructions for the Guidance of Commissioners" (1936).

"Political Memoranda for the Guidance of Commissioners
   and Other Government Officers Working in the Protectorate" (1933).

"Some Aspects of Local Government," Foreword by Sir
   Hilary Blood (1946).

"Report of the Committee on the Legislative Council Franchise," Sessional Paper #2 (1944).

"Report of the Bathurst Temporary Local Authority for the
   Year 1945," Sessional Paper #9 (1946).

"Report of the Constituency Boundaries Commission," Sessional Paper #2 (1966).

"Instructions for the Travelling Commissioners of the Gambia," West African Pamphlet #125 (1923).

### ARTICLES

Crowder, Michael.  "Chiefs in Gambia Politics," West
   Africa, Part I, 18 Oct. 1958, p. 987; Part II, 25 Oct.
   1958, p. 1017.

_____.  "Seyfou Omar M'Baki--Portrait," West Africa,
   8 April 1961.

Gailey, Harry A.  "Gambia Chiefs' Question," West Africa,
   11 March 1961, p. 255.

"Government Confers with Chiefs in the Gambia," New
   Commonwealth, 6 July 1953, pp. 27-29.

"Gambia's Critical Period," West Africa, 16 May 1964, p.
   546.

"The Last Governor," Portrait, Sir John Paul, West Africa,
   22 August 1964, p. 939.

"The Gambia's Number Two," Portrait, Sherif Sisay, West
   Africa, 31 Oct. 1964, p. 1219.

"New Voice from Africa" (Jawara), West Africa, 13 Feb.
   1965, p. 173.

"The Gambia's High Commissioners" (Louis Valentine), West
   Africa, 20 Feb. 1965, p. 197.

"Newest, Smallest: Gambia Gains Independence," _Time_, 26 Feb. 1965, p. 32.

"Toward the Gambia Republic," _West Africa_, 25 Sept., p. 1025 and 2 Oct. 1965, p. 1110.

"The Republic Rejected," _West Africa_, 4 Dec. 1965, pp. 1386-1387.

"The Gambian in Government House," Portrait, Farimang Singhateh, _West Africa_, 30 April 1966, p. 477.

## GAMBIA GOVERNMENT, SELECTED ORDINANCES

#11 (1894) Protectorate Ordinance.
The Basic government ordinance which established indirect rule in the Protectorate remained in force subject to changes by Amendment Ordinances until 1913. However, even after being officially supplanted, this Ordinance remained the key for the future theoretical development of Protectorate Administration.

#7 (1895) Protectorate Yard Tax Ordinance.
First defined a yard as the basic unit of taxation for the Protectorate and established scales of taxation.

#6 (1896) Protectorate Land Ordinance.
The basic ordinance that governed all Protectorate lands, except Public Lands, until 1945. All lands to be held by the native authorities and administered by them for the good of the people of a district.

#4 (1897) Protectorate Land (Amendment) Ordinance.
Vested the administration of Public Lands in the Chiefs and Headmen of the Protectorate.

#7 (1902) Protectorate Ordinance.
Brought Fuladugu, previously controlled by Musa Molloh, under the Protectorate system. Also extended the system to British Kombo. Otherwise the Ordinance was a repeat of #11, 1894.

#11 (1909) Protectorate (Amendment) Ordinance.
The most important amendment to #7, 1902 gave the native tribunals jurisdiction over all natives of West Africa resident in a given district.

#13 (1909) Protectorate (Amendment) Ordinance.
Main amendment concerned the appointment and regula-
tion of badge messengers for the Chiefs.

#30 (1913) Protectorate Ordinance.
Repealed all previous Protectorate Ordinances and con-
solidated them along with Rules and Regulations made by the
Governor in Council into one all inclusive ordinance.

#10 (1915) Protectorate (Amendment) Ordinance.
Redefined and clarified the executive powers of the chiefs
in the basic Ordinance #30, 1913.

#7 (1919) Protectorate (Amendment) Ordinance.
Introduced a new office of Deputy Head Chief and re-
fined method of appointing and removing Protectorate officials.
Also introduced a new scale of yard taxes.

#13 (1944) Protectorate Courts Ordinance.
Repealed Ordinance #5, 1935, and instituted a High
Court for the Protectorate with some power as the Supreme
Court of the Colony.   Continued a Protectorate Court in each
Division.   Established two classes of Magistrates.

#15 (1944) Protectorate (Amendment) Ordinance.
Changed title of certain territorial divisions and administrative areas.   Added the position of Senior Commissioner.

#10 (1945) Native Authority (Amendment) Ordinance.
Gave Native Authorities the power to expel non-Gambians
from the area of their jurisdiction.

#11 (1945) Protectorate (Amendment) Ordinance.
Amended Protectorate Ordinance #2, 1935, to allow fines
imposed on Native Officials to be paid to the general revenue
of the Native Authority.

#13 (1945) Protectorate Treasuries Ordinance.
Established Authority of Group Treasuries.   Established
a Finance committee to manage the Treasuries.   With a paid
Treasury scribe.   Established sources of revenue for such
Treasuries provided for budget estimates and better book-
keeping.   Gave the authorities the right to impose, under
certain conditions, local rates.

#16 (1945) Protectorate Land Ordinance.
Vested all Protectorate lands in the Authorities for each

District. Established a land register and provided for leases to non-indigines.

#13 (1946) Protectorate (Amendment) Ordinance.
Amended Ordinance #2, 1935, by removing British Kombo from the Protectorate system.

#16 (1946) Education Ordinance.
Section #13 gave the Native Authorities the right to open new schools under the general supervision of the Protectorate Education Officer.

#7 (1947) Protectorate (Amendment) Ordinance.
This brought Ordinance #3, 1933 and Ordinance #2, 1935 closer together by defining "Native Authority" in terms of the definition of 1933 and by substituting "Native Authority" for Chiefs in Section 13 of Ordinance of 1935.

#10, (1947) Protectorate Treasuries (Validation) Ordinance.
No Proclamation was ever issued putting Ordinance #13, 1945 into effect. Since Treasuries had been established, it was necessary to enact this ordinance making such establishments legal.

POLITICAL: Law

Ewart, Frederick K. Notes on the Trial and Treatment of Juvenile Offenders (1944).

Gray, Sir John. Notes on Criminal Procedure in Subordinate Courts (1934).

_____, comp. A Revised Edition of the Ordinances of the Colony of the Gambia (1942).

Hopkinson, Dr. E. Notes on the Laws of the Gambia Protectorate 1885-1923 (1926).

Kingdon, Donald, comp. A Chronological Table and an Index of the Ordinances of the Colony of the Gambia, 1901-1908 (London: 1909).

Montagu, Algernon, and Francis Smith, comps. Ordinances of the Settlement on the Gambia, Passed in the Years Between the 10th August 1818 and 30 December 1885, 3 vols. (London: 1882-87).

Russell, Alexander, comp. Ordinances of the Colony of the Gambia in Force 31 July 1900, with an Appendix Containing Rules under Ordinances, 2 vols. (London: 1900).

Thompson, J. H., and Donald Kingdon, comps. The laws of the Gambia in Force on the 1st day of January 1955, 6 vols. (London: 1955).

POLITICAL: Political Parties

"P. S. N'Jie," Portrait, West Africa, 3 May 1958, p. 411.

"Training period for Gambian Politicians," New Commonwealth, June 1959, p. 410.

"Politics in the Gambia," West Africa, 21 May 1960, p. 563.

"General Election in the Gambia," New Commonwealth, Sept. 1960, p. 468.

"One Gambia Party Now Seeks Independence," New Commonwealth, Spet. 1960, p. 606.

"Gambia has a Chief Minister," New Commonwealth, May 1961, p. 328.

"Man of the People," Portrait (P. S. N'Jie), West Africa, 29 July 1961, p. 823.

"Campaigning in the Gambia," West Africa, 19 May 1962, p. 535.

"New Men in the Gambia," West Africa, 9 June 1962, p. 619.

"The Gambia--May Elections," West Africa, 23 April 1966, p. 463.

POLITICAL: Foreign Affairs

GREAT BRITAIN, PAPERS BY COMMAND

"Correspondence Respecting the Affairs of the Gambia and the Proposed Exchange with France," Cmnd. 1409 (1876).

"Petitions from the Inhabitants of the Gambia," Cmnd. 1498 (1876)

ARTICLES

"Gambia and Senegal Get Together," New Commonwealth,
    June 1961, p. 393.

"The Gambia and the OAU," West Africa, 5 June 1965, p.
    618.

"Gambia Feels Pressure from Senegal," New Commonwealth,
    Nov. 1960, p. 739.

"Gambia's Links with Her Neighbours," New Commonwealth,
    Jan. 1960, p. 57.

Harrison-Church, R. J.  "Gambia and Senegal: Senegambia,"
    Geography Magazine, Sept. 1966, pp. 339-350.

Hatton, P. H. S.  "The Gambia, the Colonial Office and the
    Opening Months of the First World War," Journal of
    African History, Vol. 7, No. 1, 1966, pp. 123-132.

Robson, P.  "Problem of Senegambia," Journal of Modern
    African Studies, Oct. 1965, pp. 393-407.

Welch, Claude E., Jr.  "Gambia and the U.N. Report,"
    West Africa, 4 July 1964, p. 741.

_____.  "Is Senegambia Any Closer," West Africa, Part
    I, 7 March 1964, p. 263; Part II, 14 March 1964, p.
    285; Part III, 21 March 1964, p. 313.

SCIENTIFIC:  Geography:

BOOKS

Dallimore, H.  A Geography of West Africa (United Society
    for Christian Literature: 1948).  See pp. 17-23 for the
    Gambia.

Jarrett, H. Reginald.  A Geography of Sierra Leone and the
    Gambia (London: 1954).  Jarrett was stationed in the
    Gambia during World War II.  This book is an outgrowth
    of his personal observations and research for the M.A.
    and Ph.D. from London University.  Although very basic,
    it is the only published geographical text on the Gambia.

Lucas, C. P.   A Historical Geography of the British
    Colonies (London: 1894).   See Vol. III for the Gambia.

Reed, F. R. C.   The Geology of the British Empire (London:
    1949).   A brief discussion of the Gambia is on pp. 218-
    219.

ARTICLES

Gordon, E.   "A Land-Use Map of Kuntaur in the Gambia,"
    Geographical Journal, Vol. 116, Nos. 4-6, 1950, pp.
    216-217.

Jarrett, H. R.   "Major Natural Regions of the Gambia,"
    Scottish Geographical Magazine, Dec. 1949, pp. 140-144.

_____.   "Geographical Regions of the Gambia," Scottish
    Geographical Magazine, Dec. 1950, pp. 163-169.

_____.   "Bathurst: Port of the Gambia River," Geography,
    May 1951, pp. 98-107.

Teague, Michael.   "The Gambia," Geographical Magazine,
    Nov. 1961, pp. 380-392.

SCIENTIFIC: Geology

Cooper, W. G. G.   "Report of a Rapid Geological Survey of
    the Gambia, British West Africa," Gold Coast Geological
    Survey Bulletin, No. 3, 1927.

Webb, Dr. R. A.   Report on Soil Research, May 1952-May
    1954 (Bathurst: 1955).

"Gambia's Mineral Development," West Africa, 21 Aug. 1954,
    p. 785.

"Ilmenite Agreement," New Commonwealth, Sept. 1954, p.
    263.

SCIENTIFIC: Medicine

Gamble, D. P.   "Infant Mortality Rates in Rural Areas in
    the Gambia Protectorate," Journal of Tropical Medicine
    and Hygiene, July 1952, pp. 145-149.

Haslett, A. W.   "West Africa Experiment" (on standard of

living at Genieri), Penguin Science News, No. 23, 1952, pp. 108-113.

Horn, D. W.  "Infant Mortality in Bathurst," Gambia Annual Medical and Sanitary Report, 1942, pp. 12-14.

Hutchinson, M. P.  "The Epidemiology of Human Trypanoso-miasis in British West Africa," Annual of Tropical Medicine and Parasitology, No. 47, 1953, pp. 156-158.

Jones, C. R.  "Report on the Medical and Health Services of the Gambia," Gambia Government, Sessional Paper #2 (1970).

McCullough, F. S., and B. O. L. Duke.  "Observations on the Potential Snail Vectors of Schistosoma Haematobium and S. Mansoni," Annual of Tropical Medicine and Para-sitology, #48, 1954, pp. 277-286.

McFadzean, J. A., and J. F. McCourt.  "Leprosy in Gam-bia, West Africa," Leprosy Review, Vol. 26, No. 2, April 1955, pp. 57-64.

McFadzean, J. A., and R. A. Webb.  "Trace Element Deficiencies in Gambia," Transactions of Royal Society of Tropical Medicine and Hygiene, No. 51, 1957, pp. 425-428.

McGregor, I. A., and D. A. Smith.  "A Health, Nutrition, and Parasitological Survey in a Rural Village (Keneba) in West Kiang, Gambia," Transactions of Royal Society of Tropical Medicine and Hygiene, Vol. 46, No. 4, 1952, pp. 403-427.

Savery, G.  "The Gambia's War on Disease," West African Review, May 1956, pp. 489-493.

SCIENTIFIC: Natural Science

Hopkinson, Dr. E.  "Birds of the Gambia," Elder Dempster Magazine, Jan. 1929, Vol. 7, pp. 129-132.

_____.  "The Ducks of the Gambia," Journal of the Royal African Society, XXXV. Jan. 1936, pp. 48-52.

Johnson, E.  "List of Vanishing Gambian Mammals," Journal of the Society for the Preservation of the Fauna of the Empire.  Part 21.  May 1937, pp. 62-66.

Clarke, J. R. "The Hippopotamus in Gambia, West Africa,"
    Journal of Mammalogy, Vol. 34, No. 3, August 1953,
    pp. 294-315.


SOCIAL:  Anthropology and Archaelogy

BOOKS

Gamble, David P.  The Wolof of the Senegambia (London:
    1957).  Gamble undoubtedly knows more of the Gambia
    than any other person.  He spent years in the Gambia,
    living and working in close proximity with the native
    people.  He speaks Mandinka and Wolof and has written
    on a variety of subjects concerned with the area.  This
    book is a revision of his doctoral dissertation and repre-
    sents more than five years' work.  It is concise, in-
    formative, and the only good anthropological study of any
    of the five major peoples living in the Gambia.

Haddon, A. C.  Wandering of Peoples (London: 1911).

ARTICLES

Ames, David.  "The Dual Function of the 'Little People' of
    the Forest in the Lives of the Wolof," Journal of Ameri-
    can Folklore, Jan.-March 1958.

_____.  "The Economic Base of Wolof Polygamy," South-
    western Journal of Anthropology, Winter 1955.

_____.  "The Selection of Mates:  Courtship and Marriage
    Among the Wolof," Bulletin de l'Institute Français d'
    Afrique Noire, No. 1-2, 1956.

_____.  "The Use of a Transitional Cloth-Money Token
    Among the Wolof," American Anthropologist, Oct. 1955.

_____.  "Belief in Witches Among the Rural Wolof of the
    Gambia," Africa, Journal of the International African
    Institute, July 1959.

Beale, P. O.  "The Stone Circles of the Gambia and the
    Senegal," Tarikh, Vol. 2, No. 2, 1968, p. 1.

Beale, P. O., and F. A. Evans.  The Anglo-Gambian Stone
    Circles Expedition, 1964-65, A Report (Bathurst: 1966).

Parker, Harry.   "Stone Circles in the Gambia," Journal of
the Royal Anthropological Institute, Vol. 53, Jan.-June
1923.

Southorn, Lady Bella.   "Mysterious stone circles of the
Gambia," Crown Colonist, 1938, pp. 309-310.   An account of a visit to a circle at Niani Maru.

SOCIAL:   Demography

Jarrett, H. R.   "Population and Settlement in the Gambia,"
Geographic Review, Oct. 1948, pp. 633-636.

GAMBIA GOVERNMENT, SPECIALIZED REPORTS

"Report of the Census Commissioner for Bathurst, 1944,"
Sessional Paper #2 (1945).

"Report of the Census Commissioner for the Colony, 1951,"
Sessional Paper #4 (1952).

"Report on the Census of the Population of the Gambia, April
1963," Sessional Paper #13 (1965).

SOCIAL:   Education

GAMBIA GOVERNMENT, SPECIALIZED REPORTS

Allen, R. C.   Education in the Gambia:   Present Organisation and Possible Future Development (1939).

Baldwin, T. H.   "Report of Commissioner Appointed to Make
Recommendations on ... Education in Gambia," Sessional
Paper #7 (1951).

Gwilliam, (Miss).   Report on the training of teachers and ways
of improving Primary education by the Assistant Education
Advisor to the Secretary of State (1953).

McMath, Dr. A. M.   "Report on Infant and Girls Education,"
Sessional Paper #4 (1943).

Weston, H. C., and F. J. Harlow.   Survey of technical and
further education, Sierra Leone and Gambia (1949).

Education Department.   Annual Report.   (Issued as Sessional
Papers of the Legislative Council.)

"Secretary of State Decisions on Dr. McMath's Short Term
for the Development of Education in Bathurst," Sessional
Paper #9 (1944).

"Conclusions Reached subsequent to S. P. #9/44 on Short
Term Proposals for Development of Education in Bathurst,
Sessional Paper #4 (1945).

"Scholarships and Financial Assistance toward the Attainment
of Higher Education Qualifications," Sessional Paper #6
(1946).

"Education Policy of the Gambian Government, 1961-65,"
Sessional Paper #1 (1965).

SOCIAL:    Religion

Anderson, J. N. D.    Islamic Law in Africa (London: 1954).
See pp. 225-248 for the Gambia.

Daly, T. C. S.    "The Problem of a Young Diocese," East
and West Review, July 1948, pp. 72-75.

Fisher, Humphrey.    "Ahmadiyya in the Gambia, French
Territories and Liberia," West Africa, 27 January 1962,
p. 93.

Haythornthwaite, W.    "The Church in the Gambia," East
and West Review, Vol. 14, 1950, pp. 122-125.

SOCIAL:    Sociology

Forde, C. D.    Report on the Need for Ethnographic and
Sociological Research in the Gambia (1945).

Jarrett, H. R.    "The Strange Farmers of the Gambia,"
Geographical Review, Oct. 1949, pp. 649-657.

Jectson, Seth.    "Njuli Boys:  Circumcision Rites in the Gambia," West African Review, Oct. 1952, p. 1035.

Rees, J. G.    "Housing in a Gambian Village," African Affairs, July 1952, pp. 230-237.

Southorn, Lady Bella.    "The Old Woman of Fattato," West
African Review, July 1938, pp. 17-18.